THE
ENNEAGRAM
AND
KABBALAH

Reading Your Soul

2ND EDITION

Rabbi Howard A. Addison

Author of *Cast in God's Image:*
Discover Your Personality Type Using the Enneagram and Kabbalah

For People of All Faiths
JEWISH LIGHT
Woodstock, Vermont

The Enneagram and Kabbalah, 2nd Edition:
Reading Your Soul

2006 First Printing, Second Edition
1998 First Edition
© 2006 & 1998 by Howard A. Addison

The Library of Congress has cataloged the first edition as follows:
Addison, Howard A., 1950–
The enneagram and kabbalah : reading your soul / by Howard A. Addison
p.   cm.
Includes bibliographical references.
ISBN 1-58023-001-6 (pb)
1. Spiritual life—Judaism. 2. Self-perception—Religious aspects—Judaism.
3. Self-actualization (Psychology)—Religious aspects—Judaism.
4. Enneagram. 5. Sefirot (Cabala) I. Title.
BM723.A33   1998
296.7—dc21   98–10641
                                                CIP

Second Edition

10 9 8 7 6 5 4 3 2 1

Manufactured in the United States of America
Cover design by Bronwen Battaglia
Text design by Sans Serif, Inc.

For People of All Faiths, All Backgrounds
Published by Jewish Lights Publishing
A Division of LongHill Partners Inc.
Sunset Farm Offices, Route 4
P.O. Box 237
Woodstock, VT 05091
Tel: (802) 457-4000   Fax: (802) 457-4004
www.jewishlights.com

Contents

Preface to the Second Edition   v
Preface to the First Edition   vii
Acknowledgments   xi

Section I
Two Diagrams of Life

1 "Where Are You?"   3

2 The Tree of Life   9

3 The Enneagram   19

4 Correlation—Being and Spirit   35

Section II
The Enneagram through the Lens of Kabbalah

5 The *Sefirot:* Type and Redemption
   through Spiritual Task   47

6 Point One: *Chochmah*—Wisdom   53

7 Point Two: *Binah*—Understanding   61

8 Point Three: *Gedulah*—Greatness   69

9 Point Four: *Tiferet*—Beauty   77

10 Point Five: *Din*—Rigor   87

11 Point Six: *Netsach*—The Enduring   97

12 Point Seven: *Hod*—Splendor   105

13   Point Eight: *Yesod*—Basic Force   115

14   Point Nine: *Shechinah*—Divine Presence   123

**Section III
Returning to God**

15   *Keter:* Divine Crown, Our Transition
     to the Divine   135

16   A Meditation on the Return to *Ayn Sof*   143

Epilogue   155

Endnotes   159

Glossary   165

Suggested Readings   169

Preface to the Second Edition

It is hard to imagine more than a decade has passed since my first excited encounters with the Enneagram and its connections to Kabbalah. I continue to marvel at the new insights that these sacred maps of the human condition reveal. It has been and remains an honor to share the wisdom of these two systems with audiences of diverse ages, cultures, and religious beliefs.

Since *The Enneagram and Kabbalah: Reading Your Soul* was first published I have had the opportunity to further explore the relationship between the Enneagram and the Kabbalistic Tree of Life, and their use in determining and understanding personality type, as described in the companion volume to this book—*Cast in God's Image: Discover Your Personality Type Using the Enneagram and Kabbalah* (Woodstock, VT: Jewish Lights Publishing, 2001). In this practical guidebook, I help readers use the wisdom of the Enneagram and Kabbalah to recognize the roots of their spiritual makeup as well as determine the personality types of the people around them. These spiritual tools help readers find meaning and gain insight into their own patterns of behavior, strengths, and weaknesses, as well as in others, and use this powerful information to strengthen and enrich their own spiritual growth and the relationships with those they love. As the workbook companion to the book you now hold in your hands, *Cast in God's Image* also includes hands-on journaling exercises and guided meditations, drawn from core imagery of Lurianic Kabbalah, to help readers determine the sacred tasks that are uniquely theirs to perform. The two books together are a powerful resource in pursuing self-fulfillment, by informing and encouraging readers to address the most important questions in life: Who am I and what am I specifically called to do in this world?

I also have had the privilege of learning from the works of other authors whose findings have enriched my own understanding of the Enneagram and Kabbalah relationship. A. H. Almaas, the creative founder of the Diamond Approach to psychospiritual growth, helped me draw sharper points of connection between the *sefirot* and the Holy Ideas through his insightful text *Facets of Unity: The Enneagram of Holy Ideas* (Berkeley, CA: Diamond Work, 1998). His colleague, Sandra Maitri, presented personality development analogues to the Kabbalistic idea of *shevirat ha kelim* (the shattering of the vessels) in her book *The Spiritual Dimension of the Enneagram: Nine Faces of the Soul* (New York: Jeremy P. Tarcher/Putnam, 2000).

Of special note is James Empereur's *The Enneagram and Spiritual Direction: Nine Paths to Spiritual Guidance* (New York: Continuum, 1997). He masterfully applied Elizabeth Liebert's stages of adult spiritual growth (Elizabeth Liebert, *Changing Life Patterns: Adult Development in Spiritual Direction* [Mahwah, NJ: Paulist Press, 1992]) to each of the Enneagram types. I continue to learn from his broad experience and profound wisdom as both an Enneagram teacher and as a spiritual guide. In this book, the correlations to the four worlds and applications of Kabbalistic spiritual practices are mine; the core insights into each type's stages of growth are basically his.

I pray that this new edition of *The Enneagram and Kabbalah: Reading Your Soul* helps those who read it to come closer to others, to the Blessed Holy One, and to themselves.

Howard A. Addison

Preface to the First Edition

As a younger man, I was thrilled by the tales of Kabbalists and Hasidic masters. I marveled at the spiritual power of their teachings and the magnetism of their personalities. Most fascinating of all were their powers of clairvoyance. Again and again, I would wonder at the abilities of people like Rabbi Yaakov Yizhak Halevi Horowitz, the nineteenth-century Seer of Lublin who could read people's souls. Supposedly he could tell by glancing at someone's forehead from which location on the Tree of Life their spirit had descended and what their destiny would be.

Years elapsed since I first pondered that aspect of Jewish mysticism, and other considerations drew my attention. Yet in February 1995 my interest in mysticism was reignited. The occasion was a Spirituality seminar sponsored by the Alban Institute, an interdenominational center near Washington, D.C., that offers continuing training for clergy and congregational leaders. There, through the tutelage of Roy Oswald, I was introduced to the Enneagram.

Two aspects of the Enneagram affected me profoundly at the seminar. The first was the Enneagram's powerful insights. In the past other methods of personality typing such as Myers-Briggs had helped me understand my own character and how it interacted with the styles of others. Learning my Enneagram number proved nothing short of transformative. To find my weakness revealed as the shadow side of my strength, to discover that what I had considered my noble accomplishments were motivated, in part, by ignoble intent was profound and changed my spiritual outlook.

The relationship between the Enneagram and

Kabbalah (Jewish mysticism) also struck me during the seminar. While the two systems are not identical, their points of correspondence seemed almost self-evident. Drawing on similar ancient and medieval sources, the nine points on the Enneagram and the ten *sefirot* (potencies) on the Tree of Life (*Etz Chayim*) each posit a correlation between the structure of reality and the soul. My subsequent reading in the history and insights of the Enneagram and Kabbalistic psychology have given ongoing confirmation to my initial impressions of a correspondence between the two systems.

At the end of the seminar, I asked Roy Oswald to recommend the best single book on the Enneagram. Without hesitation, he mentioned *The Enneagram* by Helen Palmer. I immediately purchased the book and read it cover to cover several times. In turn, I enrolled in her training seminars. Helen's teaching of the Enneagram, its personality subtypes, the levels of human consciousness and how we filter information and place our attention are deeply original. While the correlations to the Kabbalah found in this text are mine, they rely upon the pioneering work of Helen Palmer and her insightful co-teacher, Dr. David Daniels.

I wrote this book for several reasons. Academically, I am interested in the parallel development of the Enneagram and Kabbalah and their points of correspondence. My own analysis indicates that the two systems of personality should be correlated differently than they have been in the past. While allusions and references to the Kabbalah/Enneagram connection can be found in previous Enneagram literature, there is a need for greater exploration and detail. I hope that this work provides some initial steps in that direction.

Also, I believe that knowledge of the Enneagram can provide those familiar with the Kabbalah (and those who would like to be) with a powerful tool for self-knowledge, critique and transformation. Jewish tradition maintains that a sacred text can be read on four levels: *Peshat* (its historical, exoteric meaning); *Remez* (the literary and verbal allusions which link it to other passages and contexts); *D'rash,* (its sermonic lessons); and *Sod,* (its hidden sense which mystically points the way to ultimate meaning). In that text known as the human heart, the Enneagram functions on the deepest level, that of *Sod.*

People who are moved to religious inquiry want to know where to begin. Common wisdom usually counsels the reading of some introductory literature and trying some of the major spiritual practices of the faith that is under consideration. Perhaps a more personalized road would also include discovering our own personality type with its strengths and weaknesses. Such a discovery could be essential to finding our own spiritual gateway to God within the tradition we are exploring.

This book is not meant to be an extensive introduction to Kabbalah or an authoritative study of the Enneagram. Instead, its first section provides an overview of both systems and insights on points of correspondence between the two. The second section examines through the lens of Kabbalah the dynamics and characteristics of the nine personality types and suggests some introductory Jewish observances that should appeal to each. It will then offer some advanced spiritual tasks appropriate for the growth of each type as prescribed by the sixteenth-century mystic Rabbi Moshe Cordevero. These religious practices were set forth as ways in which the seeker could identify with the qualities of each *sefirah.* My own interpretation of his prescriptions led me to the conclusion that the tasks for each *sefirah* are indeed appropriate for its corresponding Enneagram personality type.

It is my prayer that the insights which follow combined with the specified practices of worship, study, and loving deeds will help open the gateway to self-awareness while pointing us personally toward our own heaven's door.

Howard A. Addison

Acknowledgments

All materials in this text which describe the shift from higher to lower consciousness, from the realm of Essence to Personality with its manifestations as subtype behavior, and the path from vice to virtue conversion, are derived from the ground-breaking Enneagram work of Helen Palmer and Dr. David Daniels.

For that, I honor and thank them.

Two Diagrams
of Life

1

"Where Are You?"

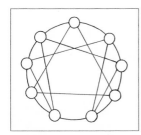EXAMINE THE FIRST CHAPTER OF Genesis and you will discover an amazing truth. In six days, God separated light from darkness, heaven from earth, dry land from the seas. Plant life and all kinds of swimming, flying and prowling creatures were called into being. However, only as the sixth day waned did God preface action with an announcement: Adam would be created in God's image and likeness. Only then did God form humans, male and female, in God's divine image.

This tale suggests that, even before we humans come into being, God knows us and calls us by name. Yet as our lives unfold, we forget our true selves and turn an increasingly deaf ear to that divine call. We grow from infancy to childhood to adolescence to adulthood developing strategies to navigate the pathways of life. We do this with greater or less success. These responses and habits become the features of our acquired personality, the face we present to the world—and even to ourselves—as we react to life's situations.

As time passes, however, we may begin feeling uneasy with our accustomed roles, with the near-scripted ways that we react to others.

Why do I always pick a fight, even before someone else has said or done anything offensive?

Is there a reason why everyone brings their troubles to me? I'm always meeting their needs, and yet I can never recognize my needs.

A sense of dissonance can develop between our acquired personalities and the "real me" which feels trapped inside and yearns to be free. We might try to take action and not know where to begin. Having become accustomed to our acquired way of being, we are unable to risk acting differently lest we lose the comfort of what we know so well. In Genesis, God called to Adam with the word *"Ayeka"* "Where are you?" Don't we, like Adam, hide from that divine call, covering our true self with the fig leaf of our rationalizations and habituated responses?

Actually, our acquired personalities are not bad things at all. Born of our own innate temperament and our perceptions and experiences, they provide us with the means to relate to other people and our environment. They cushion our essential selves from the hurt that comes from living in the world. While acting as shields and buffers, these acquired personalities can also be the starting points on our path to truth—if we recognize them. As Psalm 29 proclaims, "The voice of the Lord comes in strength." The sages of Israel interpreted this to mean that God's voice does not summon us uniformly, according to God's own strength. Instead, God calls to us individually according to our own strengths and character. Legend maintains that God's revelation at Mount Sinai was conveyed through 600,000 different channels, one for each person present. Therefore, if we seek God's personal message that is meant only for us, we might begin by learning about ourselves and our own traits.

Parallel Maps of Our Inner Universe

How can we distinguish between these acquired personality traits and the essential self hidden underneath? According to the Kabbalah, the source of each soul is rooted in a different aspect of the divine personality. The configuration of that divine personality and its ten characteristics (*sefirot*) is alternately known as *Adam Kadmon,* (the Primordial Man), or *Etz Chayim* (the Tree of Life). The search for the essential self beneath the shroud of personality might well lie in tracing back the root of each soul to its point of origin. To aid us in this quest we might call upon the Enneagram.

The Enneagram is a nine-pointed star. The origins of the diagram itself are somewhat shrouded in mystery. Some attribute its beginning to a sect of medieval Islamic mystics still in existence today known as the Sufis. Others trace its origins to the work of ancient Greek philosophers or even farther back to a Mesopotamian wisdom school in the late third millennium B.C.E. called the Sarmoun Brotherhood.[1]

Like the Tree of Life, the Enneagram is considered to depict not only the structure of ultimate reality, but also different core aspects of personality. The nine points along the Enneagram represent nine different human personality types. Each of us predominantly manifests the traits of our own particular type under normal conditions. The Enneagram is enclosed by a circle which connects the nine points around its circumference, indicating that each type might share some traits with either (or both) "Wing" points on its two sides. The points of the diagram are connected internally by lines whose distinct pattern indicates how our basic personality moves toward adopting some characteristics of another specific type when we experience undue stress and toward adopting some traits of a third type when we are feeling comfortable and secure.

As we shall see in the chapters to come, the *Etz Chayim* and the Enneagram draw upon many common historical sources and share several points of correspondence. Perhaps their most profound joint assertion is that our highest virtues and most troubling vices are actually rooted in the same source. Kabbalists have described the domain of evil as the *Sitra Achra,* literally the "Other Side" of the Tree of Life. The Enneagram teaching demonstrates how the giving person can use generosity to manipulate others or how perfectionists use the pursuit of correctness as testimony to their own superiority.

According to Jewish tradition, God fashioned human beings not with one inclination, but with two: the *Yetser HaTov* (our selfless inclination), and the *Yetser HaRa* (our self-serving, even harmful inclination).[2] Therefore, only by recognizing and confronting both sides of our creation can we begin the path toward redemption.

In Exodus, we learn that Moses climbed again to the top of Mount Sinai following the Sin of the Golden Calf and the shattering of the Ten Commandments tablets. There, Moses's skin hardened as his face began radiating power and light.[3] Afterwards, he always wore a veil while interacting with others. Only before God did Moses remove his veil, and his naked face appeared in all its toughness and its brilliance.

To get along in this world each of us, of necessity, acquires a veil of personality. This lets us interact with our world while protecting the privacy of the inner self. It can, however, become suffocating at some juncture in life. If we pull back our veils and reveal our features in all their coarseness and all their brilliance, then maybe we, like Moses, can use that revealing as the starting point for our discourse with God.

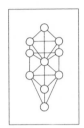

2

The Tree of Life

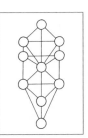THE FIRST WORD FOUND IN THE TORAH is *"Bereshit—In the beginning."* The first Hebrew letter of this first word is *"bet."* Since each Hebrew letter has a numerical value, we might have expected the first letter of scripture to be *"aleph,"* the first character in the Hebrew alphabet and the letter which equals one. Why begin the Torah with *"bet,"* which stands for the number two? While many explanations have been offered for this apparent anomaly, a Kabbalistic interpretation alludes to Creation as a dual rather than a singular process. The Creation story in Genesis is seen mystically as the outer manifestation of a more sublime unfolding. Just as our physical world was being fashioned, so the unknowable, boundless God (*Ayn Sof*) was also calling into being the configuration of God's own divine personality. This configuration, the *Etz Chayim,* (Tree of Life) is composed

of ten different characteristics. It is both the substructure, the hidden reality, of all that exists as well as the way in which God's creatures can recognize and come to know their creator.

Attempts to describe *Echad* (the One God) as subsuming ten powers actually predates Kabbalah. Early rabbinic sources not only speak of the Divine One who created the world through Ten Creative Utterances,[4] but also connect these ten utterances to the Ten Plagues and the Ten Commandments.[5] These Ten Utterances, however, are considered to be more than God's creative expressions. Their role as divine agencies instrumental in fashioning the cosmos is made explicit in a later Talmudic text.[6]

Because of its mysterious nature, many different explanations can be found in Kabbalistic literature describing the relationship between the boundless, unknowable God, *Ayn Sof,* and the ten characteristics of the divine personality, *the sefirot.* Some see the *sefirot* as merely ten different external features of the *Ayn Sof* itself, like a jewel and its facets. Others view them as ten instruments of divine power or as ten receptacles of *Shefa,* the divine radiant energy which emanates from *Ayn Sof* toward our world.

The *sefirot* are also known as God's Crowns or the names God calls Godself. The configuration of the *sefirot* has been depicted in a variety of tree, human, and geometric shapes. Mystical thinkers even differ over the numbering of the *sefirot.*

The following is a short synopsis of the *sefirot* and a common diagram of the *Etz Chayim:*

Keter   Supernal Crown, the point of transition from potential to actuality, from *Ayn Sof* to the *Etz Chayim.* It can be compared to the initial point where pen touches paper before writing begins, like the jot on top of the *Yod* (ʾ) the first Hebrew letter of the Tetragramaton (YHWH), the four-letter name of God.

Chochmah Wisdom, also known as Supernal Father, *Abba*. Encapsulated within it are the encoded archetypes of all being.

Binah Understanding, also called *Ima*, Supernal Mother. Being differentiates and unfolds within *Binah* the way the zygote develops into the various organs and limbs of the fetus in the womb.

Gedulah Greatness or *Chesed,* "Kindness," which is the creative force of God's love.

Din Judgment or *Gevurah,* "Power." This is the aspect of God that sets limits and boundaries. *Din* is to *Chesed* as form is to content.

Tiferet Beauty that comes when *Chesed* and *Din* are in balance.

Netsach The eternal, enduring nature of God, which filters the divine grace of *Gedulah* and steadfastly channels that expansive, creative energy to the lower world.

Hod Divine splendor that refracts and conveys the defining energy of *Din* to the lower world, keeping the forces of chaos and entropy at bay.

Yesod Foundation, alternately called *Tsadik* (Righteous) for the "righteous are the foundation of the world" (Proverbs 10:25). When the ten *sefirot* are depicted in human form, *Yesod* corresponds to the male generative organ, since it focuses the *Shefa's* potency from the upper *sefirot* and emits it downward.

Shechinah God's Indwelling Presence or Nearness. Like *Binah,* it is a feminine aspect of God, and

DIAGRAM 1

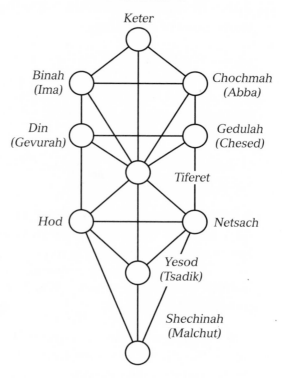

receives the *Shefa* from *Yesod* and *Tiferet* above. Pictured as bride or sister, *Shechinah* is the *sefirah* closest to our physical world. It is also known as *Malchut* (God's sovereignty).

The relationship among the *sefirot* is anything but static, and their connection to our world is hardly simple. The divine radiance of *Shefa* races back and forth among the various *sefirot,* whose balance is quite precarious. This process, known as *Ratso Va Shov* "Egress and Return," proceeds in a lightening bolt, zigzag fashion along twenty-two paths (see Diagram 1) that correspond to the number of letters in the Hebrew *aleph-bet. Sefer Yetsirah,* an early

Jewish mystical work, considered the number ten, which corresponds to the prime numbers in the decimal system, and the twenty-two letters of Hebrew, the language of God's Ten Creative Utterances, to have played an instrumental role in God's creation of the world.

Ancient physics maintained that the four essential elements of our world—fire, air, water, and earth—form a chain of ever-increasing physical density. So the Kabbalistic schema posits the descent of our physical world from the pure radiance of *Ayn Sof* as gravitating down through the *Arba Olamot* (the four worlds) of successively diminished divine light and increasing coarseness. The first, *Olam Ha'atsilut* (the World of Divine Emanation), is the dimension in which the *sefirot* initially appear though they are thoroughly integrated one with the other.

The second, *Olam Ha Beriah* (the World of Creating), marks the beginning of the *sefirot* as separate, but intimately connected, facets of the Holy. It is pictured as the realm of *Merkavah* (God's Chariot Throne [Ezekiel 1]) and the vehicle that expresses Divine Presence and concern throughout existence.

The third, *Olam Ha Yetsirah* (the World of Formation), is the world of differentiated forces and powers, personified as the various angels. This is the realm of articulation and speech.

Finally, *Olam Ha'asiyah* (the archetype of our World of Material Action) is the dimension of the greatest externality and separation, of disparate physical entities and beings, of either/or—the realm in which the Divine is the most hidden and obscure.[7]

Each of these worlds is undergirded by its own representation of the *Etz Chayim*. In descending order, the worlds and their Trees of Life are successively contracted, with the final *sefirah*, *Shechinah*, of the preceding world's *Etz Chayim*, serving as the first *sefirah*, *Keter*, of the next world's *Etz Chayim*. In ascending order the relationship of the four worlds to each other might be understood as

DIAGRAM 2

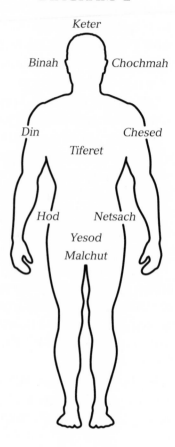

something like Russian nesting dolls in reverse. The outer doll would be the smallest; when revealed, each successive inner doll would be progressively more expansive, subsuming its predecessor.[8]

Kabbalistic Psychology

Rabbinic lore claims that before the Fall, Adam was an ethereal human-shaped creature who was so immense that he straddled the earth from one end to the other. This vast cosmic being was known as *Adam Kadmon,* Primordial Man. But with the Fall, this spiritlike individual lost its aura, became a physical creature, and was reduced to human proportions. This downsized mortal was then called *Adam Rishon,* the First Man of the later Genesis tales.

Given the Torah's depiction of God's features and emotions in personal terms and given its claim that people were created in God's image, it is hardly surprising that Jewish mystics depicted the Divine in terms of the human figure. *Shiur Komah,* a second- to sixth-century C.E. mystical movement, produced literature describing God's appearance. Reading Song of Songs as an allegory of God's love for Israel, *Shiur Komah* described God's features as being identical to those of the Song's lover, only of mammoth size. Later Kabbalists adapted the figure of *Adam Kadmon,* the cosmic-sized Adam, as an alternative to the *Etz Chayim* for depicting the configuration of the ten *sefirot.* Since Genesis tells us that God created Adam as both male and female, the *Adam Kadmon* of the *sefirot* is male and female joined in coitus.

Just as the *sefirot* form the substructure of the cosmos, they also underlie what we are as human beings. As the worldly embodiments of Adam, our psyches contain all the potentialities of *Adam Kadmon.* The interaction of the various *sefirot* engender different aspects of our psyche's function. Our creature vitality (*Nefesh*), which we share in common with the animal world, emanates from the last *sefirah, Shechinah* or *Malchut.* Since its seat is in the lower abdominal region, perhaps this is why we refer to our unconscious survival instincts as "gut feelings."

When this *sefirah* interacts with the heart-centered *Tiferet,* the social and emotional inner self of *Ruah* arises, which lifts us beyond our purely vitalistic side. *Neshamah,* which is born of the head-centered *Binah,* is both our speculative reason and the intuitive power of mind and soul which directly connects us to God. Interestingly,

Neshamah literally translates as "breath," and it is through meditative breath exercise and prayer that we can summon our higher observing mind. Detached from worldly distractions, it enables us to sense that our essential self is different from our perceptions and automatic emotional responses. It is at this level of *Neshamah* that our souls have the possibility of bonding with the Divine. Based on the notion that each human is a microcosm, later Kabbalistic psychology correlated these functions to the *Arba Olamot*, the four worlds described earlier: *Olam Ha'asiyah* represents creaturely instinct and external behavior; *Olam Ha Yetsirah*, our deeper emotions; *Olam Ha Beriah*, thought, reflection, and our initial connection to transcendence; and *Olam Ha'atsilut*, the soul.

If we each share *Adam Kadmon*'s potencies, how do we derive our individuality? Three different phenomena account for this. In a Kabbalistic reading of the Fall, Adam's sin laid in detaching *Malchut*, God's earthly presence and the lowest *sefirah*, from the rest of the Tree of Life. The reason was that Adam mistakenly considered *Malchut* to be the whole of divinity. Through this act of Adam, our lower will parted from the Divine, the uninterrupted communion of the *sefirot* with one another was severed, and a multiplicity of worlds and creatures and souls proliferated.

While each of us has all the *sefirotic* potentialities, the root of our individual souls comes from the individual *sefirot* that originate on the Tree of Life. Various biblical heroes were seen as the living embodiments of their particular *sefirah*. These include: Abraham as *Gedulah*, Isaac as *Din*, Jacob as *Tiferet*, Moses as *Netsach*, Aaron as *Hod*, Joseph as *Yesod*, and David or the matriarch Rachel as *Malchut* or *Shechinah*. The only soul to descend from *Keter* of the highest world, *Olam Ha'atzilut*, is the spirit of the Messiah who has yet to come.

The final stamp of our individuality is our acquired personality, known as *Tselem*. *Tselem* is envisioned as if it were an ethereal body serving as an intermediary between our soul and our physical being. Developed over our entire life as we interact with family, community and environment, our *Tselem* is similar to a "garment" of characteristics and traits which we weave through everything we do. Like a personal intertwining of the two *yetsers,* it is woven not only of the bright side of our virtues but also contains the *Tsel* (the truncated shadow side of those same traits that are our vices). Only the adept were capable of recognizing an individual's *Tselem* and seeing past it to the root of that soul and its place of origin on the *Etz Chayim*.

Just as all reality departed from the One, so will all reality ultimately return to the One. Each human life is a key turning point in that cycle, since each soul can perform *tikkunim.* It can repair fissures in our fragmented world which only that spirit, because of its essence and origin, can perform. Once a soul has completed its task, it ascends to its root *sefirah* on the *Etz Chayim.* When all souls perform their repairs, when all sparks of holiness (*Netsotsot*) have been elevated heavenward, then our fragmented physical existence will be redeemed and transformed back into the seamless spiritual unity of *Echad*.

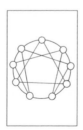

3

The Enneagram

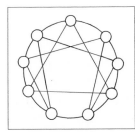 THE TERM *ENNEAGRAM* IS TAKEN from the Greek and can be translated as "nine points." This starlike diagram has been used to chart the unfolding of both cosmic processes and the human psyche. We might best understand its operation as the joining together of two ancient laws of numerical progression, the Law of the Triad and the Law of the Octave.

Simply stated, the Law of the Triad indicates that every event in our world derives from the interplay of three forces: the active force that initiates a movement; the receptive force that processes that initial action; and the reconciling force that balances the first two so that a new reality might be known. The movement of our world from simple wholeness to its current state of multiplicity might even be seen as a continuing embodiment of the triad law. In this scenario, Primary Unity, or the One, is split in two in much the way that a single cell organism splits through the biological process of mitosis. The balance needed to creatively harmonize the new relationship of these two is represented by the number three. This process is apparent in the movement from thesis to antithesis to synthesis, in the creative interaction between positive and negative electrical poles, between force and form, between male and female, all of which require a third reconciling factor to bring them such a relationship that a new actuality can come forth.

The Law of the Octave is known to us from music. If a single vibrating string is divided into eight sections by interposing seven frets along it, the change in vibration from one section to the next will increase in a precise mathematical ratio. Although the pitch of each successive note sounds higher, each incrementally shortened segment of string exhibits greater tension, decreased flexibility, and less movement than its predecessor. The increasing number of vibrations become more and more densely packed into ever shorter segments of the string. This model was used to describe the progression of reality from the spiritually simple, relaxed, and dynamic unity of the Divine to the divided, compound, restrained, static coarseness of physical being. The mathematician Francesco Giorgi described this analogy in his sixteenth-century work, *De Harmonia Mundi* (*On the Harmony of the World*).[10]

Ramon Lull, an occultist who lived in the thirteenth century on Majorca, designed a series of symbolic diagrams in which the number nine represented principles that govern the universe. Drawing upon the earlier work of Giorgi, the Jesuit Athanasius Kircher drew the Ennead in the seventeenth century as three equilateral triangles laid one upon the other (Diagram 3). Each successive triangle represented a descending class of three angels, who were seen in Christianity as intermediaries between God and the world.[11] (The three classes of angels are:

DIAGRAM 3

Seraphim, Cherubim and Thrones; Dominions, Powers and Virtues; Principalities, Archangels and Angels.)

The Armenian-born philosopher George I. Gurdjieff (1877–1949) is credited with introducing the Enneagram to the West. His search for spiritual meaning took him throughout the Middle East and into India. While his writings do not clearly indicate exactly when he learned of the Enneagram, this probably occurred during his travels at the beginning of the twentieth century. Upon returning to Europe he began teaching spirituality and psychology in Moscow and St. Petersburg. He left Russia before the 1919 Revolution, and ultimately migrated near Paris where he opened the Institute for the Harmonious Development of Man.[12]

Unlike Kircher's Enneagram, the diagram taught by Gurdjieff (Diagram 4) has only one self-contained triangle. Gurdjieff compared this enclosed equilateral triangle to the Divine, which is perfect but static. The other six points in Gurdjieff's diagram are connected by a line that runs in a sequence of points 1-4-2-8-5-7 and back to point 1. This sequence is based on the recurring decimal that occurs

DIAGRAM 4

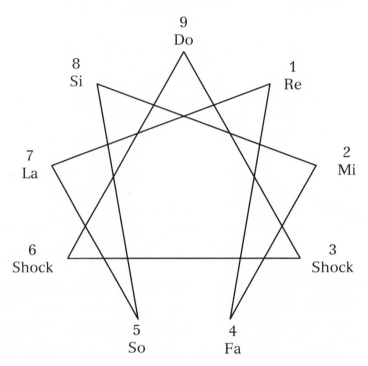

when you divide the number seven, equalling the frets in an octave, into One, signifying the original cosmic unity represented by the single vibrating string (i.e. 1 ÷ 7=.1428571428571 ...) According to Gurdjieff, this constantly moving pattern represents the dynamic movement of our changing world, with both its continuing rhythms and its need for infusions or shocks of new energy to keep our systems and life from ultimately shutting down.

The recurring decimal pattern connecting the two lower triangles shows the contribution which medieval Islamic mathematics, with its discovery of zero, the decimal system as we know it and these recurring decimals sequences, had upon the Enneagram. Although Gurdjieff attributed the ultimate origin of the symbol to the ancient Sarmoun Brotherhood, it is highly probable that some Sufi orders did transmit to future generations the Enneagram with its Islamic mathematical influences.[13]

Enneagram Theories of Personality

Like the Adam tales, the narrative that underlies the Enneagram theory of personality presupposes both Original Rightness and a Fall. Each of us is born with our own innate dispositions and an essential trust in our surroundings. When we feel at one with the world, we act with innocence, experiencing no conflicts between our thoughts, instincts and emotions. Having established no boundaries, all the potentials of the world are ours.[14]

As a child grows, he or she inevitably experiences the stresses present in any family situation and the wounds that come just from living in this material world. To survive, the child develops a separate sense of self, setting boundaries to protect and defend her essence, particularly that aspect which she feels is most threatened. Given our particular combination of temperament and experience, a filtering of our perspective occurs and almost reflexively we focus on certain data to protect ourselves where we feel most vulnerable. Our point of view gradually narrows and our range of options and responses becomes limited.[15]

The aspect of our idyllic existence which we feel we have lost, which is that particular aspect of essence that we feel is most vulnerable, is referred to in Enneagram terms as our Holy Idea. The mental image that we form of how to hide our particular weakness is called our Fixation. Our Passion is that chief emotional trait which arises to compensate for that element of essence we have lost. Our Passion which drives the development of our "script," our pattern of thoughts, feelings, and responses that lets us navigate through life, is known in Enneagram terms as our acquired personality. For each type, this pattern willfully mimics the Holy Idea. If reality will not freely provide us with that needed facet of life, we will just have to provide the gifts of that Holy Idea—or, more accurately, a restrictive, unsatisfying imitation of it—for ourselves.

In Chapter One, I indicated that the points on the Enneagram represent nine different personality types. Let me illustrate the process of personality formation by describing how it unfolds for my own personality type: the Achiever, Point Three. As a very young child, the Three lives with the Holy Idea of Hope that the world is good, that one is loved for who one is and that positive things can occur even when you don't make them happen. Because of a combination of circumstances that might include a demanding family, an unpleasant appearance and a rash temperament, the Three discovers that love and acceptance come not because of who you are, but instead are gained by what you do and how successfully you do it.[16] To compensate, the Three tries to create his own hope through preoccupation with accomplishment and status, with the Fixation of maintaining a winning Image so that others might grant their unstinting approval. The Three's perspective becomes almost instinctively focused on future tasks to perform (the more the better) and how to do these to gain prestige for himself and accolades from others, without which the Three might feel that his world will fall apart.

A Three who is a former professional athlete perfectly described this personality orientation. He stated that during his playing days he was constantly being evaluated by the coaches, the media, and the fans. Now, when he does not receive the constant appraisal of others, he feels as if "nothing is going on." Rather than risk the possibility of failure or recrimination, he'll just move on and do something else rather than stay with a task at which he is not doing well. When asked about his feelings, he replied half-jokingly, "We'll get to those later." Even the joy of victory is fleeting to him because "you're always looking forward to the next game." When it was pointed out to him that it seems as if he seeks all his validation from others rather than from inside himself, he simply stated, "external validation, that's my source of survival."[17]

But while compensating for lost Hope, the Three develops a Passion for Deceit. This Passion can manifest itself in portraying an image of being more successful and busy than he really is, of cutting corners to achieve more, and of massaging the truth so that a defeat might appear to be a "half victory." Internally, the Three deceives himself by rationalizing shortcomings as being the fault of others or circumstance and dodges his own feelings and inner reflections by moving on to the next task even if the current one is not yet completed. While the Three can be a most effective, enthusiastic leader, he can also be perceived as superficial, if not artificial, and concerned more with achieving status than with the sensitivities of others.

Characterizations of Personality

During his lifetime, Gurdjieff did not link his teaching about personality type to the Enneagram symbol. It was Oscar Ichazo, born in 1931, who used his vast knowledge of Western spiritual and philosophical traditions to originate the Enneagram of personality types. The founder of the Arica Institute in Arica, Chile, Ichazo assigned each of the Nine Passions to its appropriate point on the Enneagram. He derived the nine passions by adding a generic passion, fear, to the eight evil thoughts or orientations of mind: anger, pride, vainglory, envy, greed, gluttony, lust, and sloth which were first enumerated by the Desert Father Evagrius of Pontus (399 CE) in his *Praktikos*. These eight temptations were conflated by later Christian writers into the seven deadly sins.[18] Diagram 5 places each of the Nine Passions together with its corresponding fixation at its own Enneagram point.

The following is a short synopsis of each personality type:

Ones: Perfectionists who constantly strive to excel. Seeking to avoid criticism, they become good boys and

DIAGRAM 5

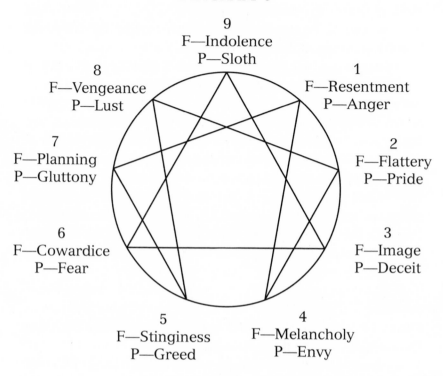

9
F—Indolence
P—Sloth

8
F—Vengeance
P—Lust

1
F—Resentment
P—Anger

7
F—Planning
P—Gluttony

2
F—Flattery
P—Pride

6
F—Cowardice
P—Fear

3
F—Image
P—Deceit

5
F—Stinginess
P—Greed

4
F—Melancholy
P—Envy

girls, internalizing their parents' standards while ever monitoring their own behavior for needed improvement. They are idealistic, objective and conscientious, but can display self-righteous anger and be judgmental and rigid with others and themselves. Concerned with order and correctness, they will usually reserve one area of life as a "trap door," a secret activity to release their suppressed chaotic impulses.

Twos: Caregivers. From an early age they learn that their sense of worth depends upon the endorsement of others. Friendly, empathetic, and generous, they flatter others for approval and adapt their personality to meet others' desires while ignoring their own. Twos take pride in making themselves indispensable. They manipulate through their helpfulness and become deflated, if not vindictive, when their efforts go unappreciated. Twos often present themselves differently to different people and may keep their friends separate from each other.

Threes: Achievers who work hard for recognition and prestige. To them, achievement ensures love. Energetic, pragmatic, and competitive, Threes may sacrifice depth and relationships to attain status and results. Enthusiastic leaders, Threes avoid failure and deceive themselves and others by exaggerating their efforts and "polishing" their defeats to maintain a winning image.

Fours: Romantics. Fashioned by memories of being forsaken by loved ones, Fours seem preoccupied with loss. They focus on the best of what's absent and the deficiencies of what's available. Sensitive, introspective, given to melancholy and shifts of mood, Fours appreciate the artistic and the unique. They avoid the mundane and strive to be perceived as "classy." Living with passionate feelings, Fours envy the lost and the unattainable while drawing their energy from romantic longing.

Fives: Observers who view life from a safe distance. They find the outside world to be intrusive and threatening. Detached, rational and outwardly unemotional, Fives are knowledgeable, insightful and comfortable analyzing abstract ideas, universal principles and group dynamics. Their greed, born from hoarding their ego resources, keeps them from sharing and commitment, while letting them be independent people of modest needs.

Sixes: Because they view the world as a fearful place, they are seen as both Loyalists and Cynics. They look for security in group activities and rules, yet maintain suspicion about the motives of others. The Phobic Six deals with fear by withdrawing from perceived threats and being cautious; the Counter-Phobic Six confronts fear by rushing headlong into challenging situations. Sixes can be wonderful team players, sacrificing heroically for a friend or a mission, while remaining cynical about the intentions of those in charge. Indecisive when insecure, Sixes can fall prey to reactionary movements that offer simple answers to difficult questions, ruthlessly justifying anything for the sake of the cause.

Sevens: Always avoiding pain, these Adventurers hide life's dark side by painting a happy face upon the world. Joyous, spontaneous, possessing a host of interests and abilities, Sevens are gluttons for pleasure. Optimistic, looking to the bright side of present situations and future possibilities, Sevens have trouble with limits and follow-through and may even use alcohol or substance addiction as a refuge from hurt.

Eights: Confrontationists who lust for power and control. To them, respect comes from strength and rejection from weakness. Eights are "bad" boys and girls who seek to dominate situations through confrontation. Assertive, forceful, unsubmitting, Eights learn to respect those who stand up to them and can be strong leaders, especially in the fight against perceived injustice.

Nines: Easy-going, patient and accepting, Nines are Mediators who seek peace by harmonizing differences between others. Seeing others' needs as more important than their own, Nines felt ignored as children and are usually surprised when they are noticed. Nines can appear slothful and lazy because they are not always focused or self-starters and are often ambivalent. Rather than say "no," a Nine might simply not act or become stubborn and passively aggressive. Once having settled on a path, however, Nines can achieve well and be excellent conciliators and counselors because of their humility, simple decisiveness and desire for unity and minimizing conflict.

The Interplay of Triads

We all relate to the world by instinct, by feeling and by thinking. Yet each of us, as a result of our own personalities, emphasize one of these faculties over the other two. These differences arise through the interaction of our innate individual temperaments with what Freud described as perceived breaks in physical/emotional "holding environments" provided for us by those serving in the parental role during the earliest stages of our development as infants.[19] The nine personality types are actually set along the Enneagram in three groups of three, each according to its own predominant faculty. These three groups are referred to as the triads.

Points One, Nine, and Eight compose the *instinctual triad*, those whose temperaments made them particularly sensitive to the earliest stage of the separation-individuation process, the break experienced by first sensing that one is a separate body and self. People in this group indicate that they will actually experience bodily sensations when a new situation occurs before they are able to identify what they are thinking or feeling. Because these sensations often are experienced in the abdominal region as "gut feelings," it seems as if the belly has an intelligence of its own. The energy of these *"Belly Centered"* types is the energy to "stand against," which is manifested by the aggressiveness of the Eight, the stubbornness of the Nine, and the critical perfectionism of the One.

Seven, Six, and Five are the thinking types, the *"Head Centered"* triad. Their temperaments rendered them vulnerable to any perceived inability of their caregivers to adequately recognize or respond to their physical survival needs—to be fed, changed, and sheltered. This break in their infantile "holding environments" led these types to experience the world as a limiting (Sevens), fearful (Sixes), or an intrusive (Fives) place. Their energy seems to move inward: the Seven withdraws from current commitment and activities in the ongoing search for new stimulation; the Six cautiously pulls back before either escaping from a perceived threat or rushing into it; and the Five reclusively isolates himself in thought.

The *feeling triad*, types Four, Three, and Two, felt a

lack of emotional attunement in their infantile "holding environments." Their primary caregivers seemed unable to adequately perceive, value, or mirror back their feelings, the depth of who they are. They are called the *"Heart Centered"* types because the heart is traditionally seen as the seat of their predominant faculty, the emotions. The energy of these three types seems to move toward others to gauge feelings, particularly the feelings of others toward them: the Twos, who wish to be loved; the Threes, who wish to be admired; and the Fours, who wish to be understood.

An unusual feature of the Enneagram is that the center type of each triad, located at the three core points on the enclosed triangle, actually appears to repress its triad's own dominant faculty. If the Eight externalizes her instinctual responses by being aggressive and the One internalizes them by becoming self-critical, the Nine seems almost out of touch with instinct and incapable of moving decisively to action. While the Two externalizes emotion so that he can sense even the unspoken needs of others, and the Four internalizes feeling to the extent that he becomes moody and brooding, the Three holds back his feelings lest they interrupt his drive for achievement and success. Similarly, if Fives internalize their thinking to the point of self-isolation and Sevens externalize their thoughts by always planning for exciting future possibilities, the Sixes' thinking can become paralyzed by doubt and thoughts of potential danger that have no connection to reality.

Rather than being the prime example of their triad's predominate faculty, the respective core types might not outwardly show that trait at all. The Nine can seem the least instinctive, the Three the least feeling, and the Six the least thoughtful of all types.

The Dynamics of Types

Our individual personality types are not a static collection of habits and traits. Diagram 6 provides us with a key to

DIAGRAM 6

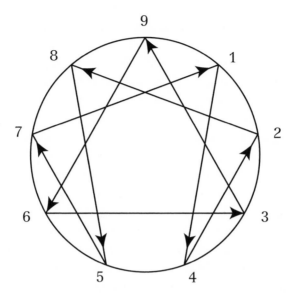

understanding how your own type might interact with other types and even assume some of their characteristics.

The circle connecting the points around the circumference indicates the connection which adjacent numbers have to each other. The neighboring numbers on each side of a point are referred to as that point's "Wings." Both Wings will affect the type, on each side of it, though in every individual one Wing will predominate, giving that personality a distinctive slant. A Two who is a caregiver, for example, might lean either toward the One and be more concerned with order and correctness or toward the Three and be inclined to strive for success to gain recognition and prestige.[20]

Highly important in differentiating personalities within the same type is the use of Instinctual Subtype. As mentioned above, while some of us relate to the world primarily through thinking or feeling, we all possess instincts that help us survive. As with other animals, our survival instincts manifest themselves as three different drives: A drive for self-preservation; a sexual drive that leads to intimacy and propagation of the species; and a social drive to fit in with the group, to maintain the herd. While each of us is sensitive to all three, we are predominantly concerned with the one instinct that is our most vulnerable. This, in turn, will slant how the Fixation and Passion of type will play out for that person in much the same way that a person seated on a three-legged stool will slant if one stool leg is shorter than the other two. Thus, a Two who feels vulnerable in social settings might instinctively turn his attention toward those with power so that he can assure his status in the group. Another Two who is uneasy about establishing intimate relationships might be aggressively flirtatious, while a third Two who is concerned with preserving his own well-being might insist that, since he does so much for others, he should receive preferential treatment.[21]

The arrows along the lines connecting the points to each other represent another sort of interaction among the types. In addition to our predominant type, which determines our conduct during normal circumstances, we tend to move toward another type when under unusual pressure and toward a third when feeling safe and comfortable. The type whose characteristics we assume when we are overwhelmed is called our Stress Point. Movement with the arrow is toward one's Stress Point, such as 1—>4. The movement against the arrow is toward one's Security Point, such as 1<—7. This is the type whose characteristics we exhibit when we feel at great ease. Thus, a One, when facing normal challenges, will exhibit more of the One fixation and become very fussy and picky and concerned with the order and correctness of what he *can* control: My world is falling apart so let me clean this room that I'm in. When facing heavier pressure, she might move to the lower features of her stress point, Four, and feel overly melancholy, maudlin and alienated. When at ease with their companions and environment, Ones can move toward the higher side of their security point, Seven, and be adventurous and playful.[22]

Return to Essence

As mentioned earlier, the Holy Idea indicates that aspect of Essence or original rightness that has been negated. This wounding leads, as we have seen, to the developing of Fixation and Passion as the ways in which the personality compensates for its loss. In the quest for personal growth, one would seek to embody the Virtue that is the opposite of and the balance for one's emotional Passion. Below is a diagram of Essence (Diagram 7) with the Holy Idea above each corresponding Virtue.[23]

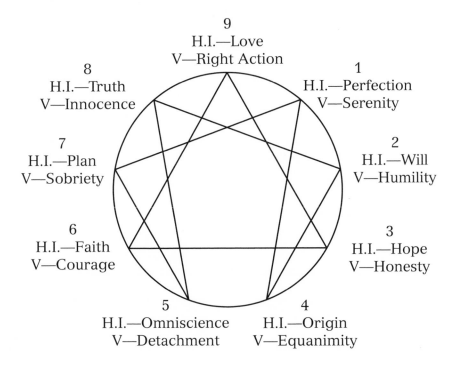

DIAGRAM 7
H.I.—Holy Idea   V—Virtue

9
H.I.—Love
V—Right Action

8
H.I.—Truth
V—Innocence

1
H.I.—Perfection
V—Serenity

7
H.I.—Plan
V—Sobriety

2
H.I.—Will
V—Humility

6
H.I.—Faith
V—Courage

3
H.I.—Hope
V—Honesty

5
H.I.—Omniscience
V—Detachment

4
H.I.—Origin
V—Equanimity

While the second half of this book will address the interplay of Essence, Personality and the spiritual task appropriate to each type, let us return for the sake of example to the Three. This type has lost essential Hope that the world is good, that one is loved and that needs are met independent of one's achievement. He fixates on the Vanity of maintaining a winning image and will Deceive others and himself to appear successful and gain accolades and prestige. (See Diagram 5.) To achieve spiritual growth and reclaim a measure of his essential lost Hope, the Three must begin by Honestly examining himself and taking responsibility for his misrepresentations, rationalizations, and failures.

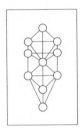

4

Correlation—
Being and Spirit

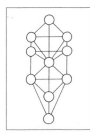 SEVERAL POINTS CONNECT THE KABBAL-
istic system of the *sefirot* and the Enneagram,
especially since theories of being in both
begin with an Essential One which unfolds
into multiple characteristics. Both the
ten-aspect Tree of Life and the nine-pointed
Enneagram posit dynamic internal interaction
within the system—what Gurdjieff called "perpetual motion" and Kabbalah terms *Ratso Vashov,* "Egress and
Return."

In the realm of personality, both the Enneagram and
Kabbalah claim that although all psyches potentially embody all the potencies, each manifests a predominant type
or derives from a particular *sefirah.* Just as the Enneagram
speaks of an acquired personality with its interrelated
light and dark sides, so does Kabbalah describe the *Tselem*
(the ethereal "garment" of our traits and experiences

which we develop over our lifetime) which inevitably includes its truncated shadow side (*Tsel*). Just as Kabbalah divides our souls into *Nefesh, Ruah,* and *Neshama,* the Enneagram also details three centers of intelligence: the Belly, which is instinctually concerned with our physical survival; the Heart, which is our emotional core; and the Head, which is our mental center.

Finally, both systems speak of shatterings, different levels of reality, and a restorative, redemptive process. Kabbalah speaks of *shevirat ha kelim,* the shattering of the seven lower *sefirot* because they could not successfully contain the *Shefa*. It also speaks of the descent of reality through the four worlds (*Arba Olamot*) and the scattering of the *Netsotsot* (sparks of Divine radiance) throughout the world. It is the task of each individual to elevate the *Netsotsot* of our own *sefirah* so that these sparks—and ultimately each individual's soul—might return to its rightful home in the Tree of Life. The Enneagram speaks of more personal shatterings, beginning in infancy with the first perceived breaks in our "holding environments," when we begin to lose that aspect of Essence which is our Holy Idea. As we mature we realize, due either to loss, setbacks, illness, or perhaps just in a moment of awareness, how stifling our habits and rationalizations really are. (Perhaps the rabbinic proscription to refrain from studying Kabbalah until age forty was not merely to address the student's need for mature stability, but to give the seeker a chance to acquire the existential openness that only comes from life's brokenness and examining our values and goals in middle age.)

If idolatry is worshipping our own creations as a substitute for God, then the acquired personalities we have fashioned to imitate our type's lost aspect of Essence are, in effect, our own inner idols. As the Hasidic master Moshe of Kobrin stated, it is the "I" that stands between us and the Divine.[24] By moving from our Fixation and its corresponding Passion toward our Virtue, we can transcend our subservience to this inner idolatry, reconnect with the Holy Idea of Essence, and feel at home with existence.

If Kabbalah asserts the existence of four worlds descending from the ultimate reality of *Ayn Sof,* the Enneagram personality theory can reflect four parallel ascending stages of adult spiritual growth, each uniquely manifest through the orientation of the nine different types. As described by Elizabeth Liebert in *Changing Life Patterns,* these stages are the Conformist, the Conscientious, the Interindividual, and the Integrated.[25]

The first, or Conformist, stage of growth is similar to *Olam Ha'asiyah* (World of Physical Action) in that both focus on the external and the material. Psychologically, *Olam Ha'asiyah* is the realm of separate beings, of outer conduct and appearances; the Conformist stage is reflected by concern with outward behaviors and external norms, with material thinking and either/or stereotypes. Both are the realms in which the Divine is most hidden and obscure.

Like *Olam Ha Yetsirah* (World of Formation) with its fellowship of angels and diverse forces, the Conscientious stage is based on greater mutuality in relationships and recognizing the legitimacy of different alternatives in life. On the psychological level, *Olam Ha Yetsirah* is the realm of emotions. During the Conscientious stage we become conscious of and begin to acknowledge those deeper emotions we have repressed through the fixations and passions of our acquired personalities. The articulation of that which was previously hidden and a more realized inwardness mark both these domains.

If *Olam Ha Beriah* is the realm of thought, the Interindividual stage marks the thoughtful integration of the gifts of our type with our previously repressed inner feelings. Similar to the luminous interconnection of the *sefirot* in *Olam Ha Beriah,* those at the Interindividual stage are able to harmonize inner and outer realities that, at a superficial level, might seem to conflict—to live with mystery and paradox. Better able to reflect godly concern for others in diverse social contexts, they embody in their lives the Kabbalistic dictum that each person should strive to be a *Merkavah* (God's Chariot Throne) located in *Olam Ha Beriah,* that conveys God's presence and concern to the world.[26]

The fourth stage of growth, the Integrated stage, is most likely beyond the scope of mortal achievement. If *Olam Ha'atsilut,* the highest world of Divine Emanation, is the unified realm of soul, how many individuals can or have ever approached a life of unconflicted, soul-filled wholeness? Like the total integration of all the Divine potentialities of the *sefirot* in *Olam Ha'atsilut,* the Integrated stage is marked by the seamless harmonization of intimacy, mutuality, and action in the world. While the journey from stages one through three represents a gradual refining, breaking down, and a higher reconstitution of the personality, movement toward stage four marks a deconstruction aimed at transcending the personality. Living the reality that from the standpoint of Essence our lives are not about our selves, these uniquely redeemed and redemptive individuals who most closely approach Integration embody a sense of universality. Their concern encompasses a broad scope of environmental, social, and cultural needs. Like *Olam Ha'atsilut,* their position in life is closest to the Holy, the sacred One.

A guiding axiom for those who would engage in the spiritual journey is that if you feel distant and lost, retrace your steps and go back the way you came. Therefore if our material existence descended from *Ayn Sof* through the *Arba Olamot,* the four worlds, then our path back to Essence may be marked by these four stages of spiritual growth. Like the ancient Israelites wandering through the Sinai wilderness toward the promised land, however, this journey is neither smooth nor direct. It has its stops and starts, it has progressions and regressions, its peaks, valleys, and usually long plateaus. Not everyone ascends through all the stages. While a large number of adults will move from the Conformist to the Conscientious stage, far fewer will make the transition to the Interindividual stage; those even approaching the Integrated stage are exceptional and rare.

As each of the ascending four worlds is successively more expansive, the shatterings we experience along life's path tend to break open the more limited perspective of our current stage, preparing us for the greater expansiveness and inclusiveness of the stage to come. At the journey's beginning, the Conformist/*Olam Ha'asiyah* stage, the nine types look quite different. As they depart from their disparate starting points along the Enneagram's outer circle and move upward through the successive *Olamot*/Stages, they resemble each other ever more closely as their paths converge on the road toward Essence.

Points of Juncture

In his book *Meetings with Remarkable Men,* Gurdjieff refers to a text entitled *Merkhavat.* While *Merkavah* (God's Chariot Throne) is the name of the earliest movement in Jewish mysticism, there is no known book entitled *Merkhavat.* Ichazo asserted his own ties to Jewish mysticism by claiming that the archangel Metatron revealed to him the placement of the Passions.[27] Although these passing references obscure as much as they reveal, common influences on the Kabbalah and the Enneagram derive from antiquity and medieval times. These include Pythagoreanism, Neoplatonism, Gnosticism, Christian Asceticism, and Sufism.[28] An early attempt to place the *sefirot* along the points of the Enneagram was attempted in the seventeenth century by the aforementioned Athanasius Kircher. He located three *sefirot* (*Keter, Chochmah, Binah; Gedulah, Din, Tiferet; Netsach, Hod, Yesod*) along the three self-contained triangles overlaid one on the other (Diagram 8).

When Gurdjieff opened the Enneagram's bottom two triads, the three highest *sefirot* remained at the points of the self-contained triangle. The lower six were placed along

DIAGRAM 8

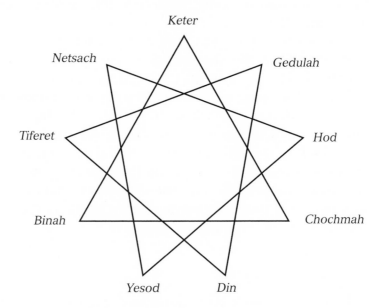

the two open, interconnected triads representing their dynamic interaction (Diagram 9). The circle joining the points symbolized *Malchut, Shechinah,* the tenth *sefirah,* representing God's Presence, which encircles the world.

When I first saw this placement of the *sefirot* along the Enneagram, it seemed somewhat out of order: *Keter,* which is the point of transition from potential to actuality, was occupying the mediating, accepting Nine point. *Yesod,* representing the assertive force of the male generative organ, was placed in the introspective, emotionally detached Five position. The configuration of the other *sefirot* seemed peculiar to me as well.

It occurred to me that this dissonance might be traced to the Kabbalistic doctrine of the four worlds. According to this doctrine our world emanates from *Ayn Sof* through four descending realms of increasing physical density. Each world has, as its underlying reality, its own represen-

DIAGRAM 9

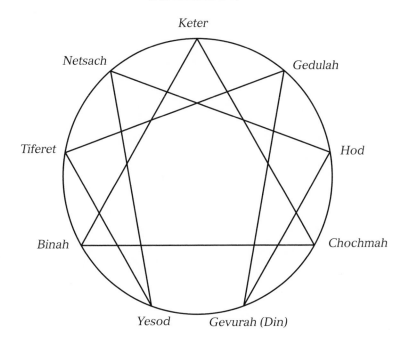

tation of the *Etz Chayim*. These Trees of Life are connected to each other by the final *sefirah, Shechinah,* of the prior Tree serving as the *Keter* of the succeeding Tree. (The relationship between these two *sefirot* is further alluded to in their names: *Keter,* "Crown," and *Malchut,* "Sovereignty." In some Kabbalistic schema, the final *sefirah* is even called *Atarah,* "Tiara.") Therefore, it would make sense that in the realm governing human personality, the fourth world (*Olam Ha'asiyah*), *Shechinah* would occupy the top position on the Enneagram.

The placement of *Shechinah* rather than *Keter* at the top position is supported by two additional facts. Since only the Messiah's soul will derive from *Keter,* no single human personality type can be rooted in that *sefirah.* Additionally, *Shechinah* accepts and harmonizes the divine

DIAGRAM 10

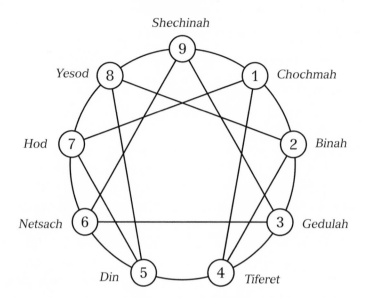

energy from the other *sefirot* in the same way that Nines accept and harmonize others' divergent points of view.

By beginning with *Shechinah* in the Nine position, Diagram 10 seems to me to be the most valid placement of the *sefirot* along the Enneagram.

The above configuration places *Keter* in the middle, hovering above the diagram as the transition from the One to the many. The other nine *sefirot* now seem to correlate more readily to the Enneagram types:

1. *Chochmah*—The all-knowing, Correct, Internalized Father, *Abba*.

2. *Binah*—The understanding, Controlling, Supernal Mother, *Ima*.

3. *Gedulah*—Impetus to be great.

4. *Tiferet*—Beauty, and Romantic Longing.

5. *Din*—Bound, Enclosed, Limited.

6. *Netsach*—Enduring, and Seeking Authority.

7. *Hod*—Splendor

8. *Yesod*—Seminal Force.

9. *Shechinah*—Accepting Presence.

Because *Din* and *Tiferet* are usually numbered four and five on lists of the *sefirot,* attempts have been made to correlate *Din* to Point Four and *Tiferet* to Point Five. As I mentioned above and will detail in the following chapters, I believe that *Tiferet* more closely corresponds to the traits of Point Four, the Romantic, and *Din* to Point Five, the Observer. Conceptually, the reason for this reversal might be Gurdjieff's opening of the Enneagram's lower two triangles (see Diagrams 3 and 4), a configuration that flipped the positions of Points Four and Five, the bottom two points on the Enneagram.[29]

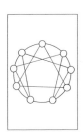

The Enneagram through the Lens of Kabbalah

The Sefirot: Type and Redemption through Spiritual Task

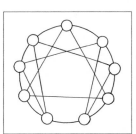

RELIGIONS CLASSICALLY DEPICT saints and sinners as having fairly specific virtues or vices. Judaism is no different. It traditionally speaks of three categories of individuals: the *Tsadik* (Righteous); the *Rashah* (Wicked); and all the rest of us, the *Benoni,* which literally means, "those hovering in the middle." A powerful insight of the Enneagram is that these categories manifest themselves differently as levels of development for each type. The vices at the low level of a Point's development are the compulsions or *Sitra Achra,* the "Other Side" of the virtues found at their higher level.[1]

In this section, we will examine each *Sefirah*/Enneagram Point. In the first paragraph of each chapter, we will set forth in bold type the names of the types, their initial specific *shevirah,* "shattering," or the basic premise of their fall from Essence or Holy Idea into the Fixation and Passion of acquired personality and how these manifest in the three *Subtypes*. We will then consider what the *Rashah* (unredeemed), *Benoni* (average), and *Tsadik* (redeemed) manifestation of each type's traits might be. While no written description can adequately depict the intricate patterns of progress, backtracking, and detours that comprise even one person's spiritual and emotional path, we will offer snapshot descriptions of the first three *Olamot/* Stages that may mark each personality type's particular journey.[2] To illustrate these Points, we will look at the profiles of those scriptural figures whom the Kabbalah considered to be the embodiments of their particular type, observing both the triumphs and pitfalls of these various biblical heroes.

For those wishing to begin the spiritual journey through Jewish observance, each chapter will suggest a different Gateway, or *Sha'ar*. As a result of their special orientations, each of these activities will have a stronger appeal for each Enneagram type. An observance or ritual that might prove particularly appealing to each type will be described for those seeking growth by connecting or reconnecting with Jewish life.

Also, a variety of different approaches have been prescribed for students of the Enneagram who seek more advanced personal growth. Among them are trying to embody the Virtue of your type, confronting and dwelling upon the characteristics which your type instinctually avoids, and trying to shift your style of behavior to manifest the higher traits of your Security Point.

To again return to our Three, if she wishes to grow she might balance her Passion for Deceit with the Virtue of Honesty by being fully truthful with others and by ruthlessly examining her feelings and her own self-deceptions. If, because of her overwhelming need to succeed, she avoids all association with failure, she must then claim responsibility for her defeats and live with their repercussions rather than portray them as partial victories or blame them on circumstances or on other people. Finally, our Three might try to exhibit the higher traits of her Security Point, Type Six, to cooperate rather than always compete with others and to show constancy in her allegiances rather than constantly shift around for the sake of expediency.

The Wisdom of Cordevero

The spiritual disciplines listed as *Tikkun*/Repair at the end of the following chapters are taken from *Tomer Devorah,* or *Deborah's Palm Tree,* written by Rabbi Moshe Cordevero and first published in Venice in 1587.[3] Cordevero, who lived in Safed in Northern Israel in the sixteenth century, was a student of the great mystical legalist Rabbi Joseph Caro. He also taught the seminal Kabbalist, Rabbi Isaac Luria.

The spiritual tasks Cordevero sets forth have two goals. The first is to help us identify with and embody the qualities found in each of the *sefirot.* As such, his disciplines lead students to manifest the *Virtue* of the given *sefirah:* sometimes by emulation; sometimes by a task that makes them confront their avoidance; and sometimes by acts that exhibit the higher qualities of their Security Point. These very concrete acts and practices can help seekers in their quest to move from the *Olam Ha'asiyah*/Conformist stage through the *Olam Ha Yetsirah*/Conscientious stage toward the higher Interindividual world of *Olam Ha Beriah.* They are also consistent with the traditional rabbinic prescription *"Lo Hamidrash Haikar Elah Hamaoseh...,"* "It is the deed and not the exposition which is essential."

Cordevero's disciplines have a second, more sublime purpose. To understand this goal better, let us revisit the *Etz Chayim* of Diagram 1.

According to Kabbalistic thought, Adam's Fall produced severe dislocations in the Tree of Life and,

DIAGRAM 1

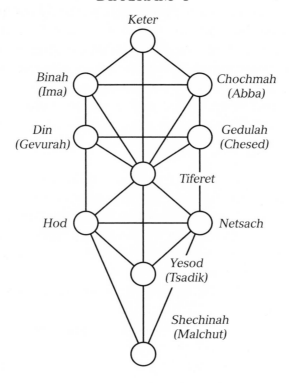

therefore, in the world. The pathways that convey the *Shefa* (the divine radiance) from *Ayn Sof* to the various *sefirot* have become misaligned, if not completely severed. *Shechinah* is in exile, cut off from the rest of the Tree. Her connection along the center pathways to *Tiferet* and *Yesod,* and their connection to each other, has been weakened and stretched. The full measure of divine energy cannot flow through the center pathways to our world below. The forces of the Left side are out of balance with those on the Right. This causes a predominance of *Din's* harsh judgments because they are not properly tempered with the mercy of *Chesed*. These blocks to the proper flow of

Shefa to the individual *sefirot* also means that during this unredeemed time, the *sefirot* themselves will exhibit lower as well as higher traits.

Because each of us is created in God's image, what we do on earth resonates in the divine sphere above. Therefore, the tasks that Cordevero detailed perform the function of *Tikkun,* of bringing needed repair to the *Etz Chayim* and the individual *sefirot.* As such, our own spiritual quest can lead us not only to self-growth, but to divine repair and world redemption.

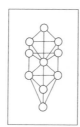

6

Point One:
Chochmah—Wisdom

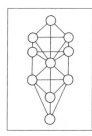

THOSE WHO OCCUPY POINT ONE ON the Enneagram are usually viewed as **Perfectionists**. By perceiving the world as a place that criticizes and penalizes wrong thought and deed, Ones have lost the Holy Idea of **Perfection**, the undivided rightness of all things. Having learned that approval comes from correcting error and being good, Ones develop a mental fixation of **Resentment** and an emotional passion of **Anger**. They deny their own desires in the face of exacting internal and external standards. On the instinctual Subtype level, the passion can manifest itself as **Jealousy**, the critical judging of one's mate's intentions in intimate situations; as **Inadaptability** in social settings; and as the **Anxiety** that comes from making a mistake and endangering one's self-preservation.

Corresponding to Point One is the *sefirah* of *Chochmah,*

or Wisdom. Like Perfection, its corresponding Holy Idea, *Chochmah* encapsulates the pristine completeness of all that is. When used, however, as a standard of perfection against which to judge reality's flaws, the Kabbalistic attribution *Chochmah* (Wisdom) is fitting; Ones can give the impression that only they have the wisdom to know fully what is correct in every situation.

PERSONALITY AND ITS TRAITS

Given their abiding commitment to principle, Ones tend to be conscientious, honest, hard-working, and responsible. They value integrity, punctuality, and precision in themselves and others. Always concerned with "doing the right thing," Ones strive for excellence and constantly seek ways to improve themselves and others. Their high moral sense can lead them to crusade for justice and truth.

Because of their temperament and upbringing, Ones are quite self-critical but have a hard time accepting criticism from others. They displace their anger by finding fault with those who violate conventional standards, and who seem to be "getting away with something." By cloaking their anger in moral self-righteousness, Ones can avoid the inner recriminations that come from having bad feelings toward others. At their most obsessive, Ones can be dogmatic, inflexible, and even cruel toward those who don't do what they know is right. Ones have described this orientation as:

> "I never feel acceptable so I strive to be perfect so I won't be cast aside ..." "The search for security lies in getting things right ..." "Error gets you expelled from the Garden [of Eden] and brings down the hierarchy of the world."

Ones inhabit a world of mental comparisons: Do my actions and thoughts live up to my ideal? Are others criticizing me? Is someone else ahead of me? Will I feel diminished if I compliment someone else? Caught between their desires and their sense of "should," Ones may procrastinate, wavering between doing what they want to do, which might not be correct, and doing what is correct, which isn't really what they want. Seeking what might be termed as "trapdoor release," Ones can develop a dual self. They can be proper at home, while playful on holiday, or have a meticulously clean desktop, but reserve one drawer for clutter and junk. Prim and proper, some Ones actually vacation far from home so that they can sunbathe undetected by friends or acquaintances at nude beaches.

As with all personality types, the traits that comprise the One personality manifest differently at different levels. *Tsadik,* or redeemed, One qualities appear as wisdom, integrity, conscientiousness, and a willingness to fight for justice and truth. At the *Benoni,* or moderately developed, level these same characteristics emerge as self-righteousness; the tendency to moralize; a devotion to protocol, etiquette, and rules; and the need to improve everyone else. *Rashah,* or unredeemed, One manifestations of these traits include paralysis in the quest for self-perfection, intolerance, seeing absolutes with no shades of gray, and the punitive treatment of others' mistakes as heinous crimes.

ASCENDING THROUGH THE *OLAMOT*

Conformist/*Olam Ha'asiyah* Ones seem constantly under the sway of their inner critics. This dynamic not only leads them to be judgmental of others and themselves, but also blocks access to their deeper feelings. Out of touch with the inner self they focus on externals, especially others' behavior and its acceptability according to their understanding of approved social norms. To them, injustices stem from what others "should" be doing, but are not. Their feelings of anger and resentment often blind them to the difference between the essential and the trivial, so that the violation of even the smallest protocol can seem like the betrayal of a major ethical imperative. Rather than confronting the possibility that complex situations might require flexibility in judgment, they may tend to dispel the resulting inner feelings of pressure through a "trapdoor release" as mentioned above. Finding it difficult to integrate pleasure, they need to either earn their time off or justify it by pursuing some worthwhile purpose. A moment of transition (*shevirah*) may come when Ones finally buckle under the weight of the unattainable standards they have set for themselves.

Moving into the Conscientious/*Olam Ha Yetsirah* stage, Ones start to recognize how the inner critic has repressed their deeper needs for acceptance and narrowed their scope of experience. With this recognition comes the ability to see reality as it is, rather than through the lens of constant evaluation. Ones become less judgmental, experience life more broadly, and become more comfortable with the good even if it is not perfect. Accepting their own strengths and weaknesses, they become more accepting of others, allowing for greater intimacy and pleasure in relationships. Less defensive, they are better able to confront their anger and discern what is just, what is unjust, and what are justifiable reactions to given situations. A continuing challenge for Ones at this stage is the sense that their lives have come untethered without their ongoing attachment to propriety while experiencing the fear that comes from realizing that not everything can be controlled.

Having integrated their deeper emotions with their gifts of discernment and clarity, Interindividual/*Olam Ha Beriah* Ones now exhibit greater discernment in their judgments and greater tolerance for ambiguity. Possessing a more sophisticated understanding of human dynamics, they are both kinder to themselves and able to infuse their personal relationships with a mutuality and intimacy that is both honest and loyal. Now able to recognize that their anger most likely stems from their unconscious, they can combine sensitivity toward others with playfulness and a sense of humor. Their critical ability allows them to both identify social evils in this world and offer effective solutions. What was formerly self-righteousness now manifests as a willingness to stand against convention and the crowd, if need be, to correct injustices and to protect those who are marginalized.

THE BIBLICAL HERO: *ABBA*

Kabbalists personified the *sefirah* of *Chochmah* as *Abba,* Supernal Father. In many ways, Ones seem to respond to the internalized voice of an ascendant father. This inner voice continually calls them to perfection, to do better. In effect, it states, "You'll be loved if you deserve it, if you're right."

As stated above, *Chochmah* is much like the Essence of Holy Perfection—it contains the undifferentiated, pristine ideals of all that exists. However, when in character fixation, the One's perception mimics Essence by angrily looking to the correctibility of things. Their penchant for criticism comes from measuring our flawed actuality against the yardstick of their conceived, but unrealized, ideals. "Oh, how perfect this could be" gives way to "Damn! How lacking this really is." Interestingly, Kabbalists have identified *Chochmah* with "Yod," the first Hebrew letter of God's four-letter name (YHWH). Yod looks just like a point (י) that geometrically has the potential for expansion in all three dimensions. *Chochmah,* like the point, contains the possibility for measuring and, thus, comparing all things. Organically, *Chochmah* is likened to a seed that contains all the biological information needed for the new life. However, *Chochmah* truly becomes *Abba,* Father, when it accepts in wholeness the beauty and the flaws of that which exists, while engendering that which animates and gives life.

SHA'AR/GATEWAY

Justice and righteousness are key Jewish values. The High Holy Day liturgy describes God as a "Just King" who is exalted by righteousness. The words of Isaiah, which are read on Yom Kippur, proclaim, "loose the bonds of wickedness ... and let the oppressed go free." *Aleynu* (the prayer of adoration) bids us to join in this task so that we might "perfect the world under the kingship of God."

These calls to justice and social reform match Ones' dedication to principle and quest to improve the world around them. High Holy Day worship can remind them that such striving is godly when motivated by righteous concern for others rather than by self-righteousness. Throughout the year, they can help "perfect the world" by joining with Jewish and interfaith groups whose religious principles lead them to work for a more equitable and just society.

Rosh Hashanah and Yom Kippur call each of us to examine our motivations and our deeds. While self-evaluation comes naturally to Ones, the Holy Days stress that we should undertake such activity for the sake of reconciliation. By emphasizing the urgency and frailty of human existence the Holy Days teach Ones, and all of us, that life is too short to harbor resentment. Each day of each new year is the time to look truthfully at our strengths and flaws, to admit when we are wrong, to seek the forgiveness of people we have hurt and misjudged, and to forgive and accept those who have hurt us.

TIKKUN/REPAIR

In the third chapter of his *Tomer Devorah,* Cordevero addresses the path of growth associated with *Chochmah:* "How should one act to become accustomed to the divine quality of *Chochmah* ... be ready to give beneficial teaching to all, to each according to that individual's ability to understand."

Ones who seek further spiritual growth must begin by softening the harshness of their principles and standards by recognizing that positive change can only come when you teach others for their benefit, not when you criticize them to enhance your own feelings of validation.

If Anger is the Passion of Ones, then *Serenity* is One's Virtue. To achieve serenity, Cordevero counsels daily time for each of us to be engaged in "contemplation in solitude upon [his] Creator." In that way, wisdom can be realized by calming the passions and acknowledging that perfection lies only with God and not in unattainable absolutes. The divine balancing of judgment with compassion, of life's expansive and constricting traits, is how Ones, and all others, can achieve wholeness.

The Enneagram indicates that One's Security Point is Seven, the point of joy and vitality. Cordevero calls Ones to embrace the higher traits of vivaciousness "to teach life to the world ... [to] spout forth life toward all things." If Ones are judgmental and disdain the unconventional while seeking only stable "worthwhile" companions, Cordevero encourages them to "bring back the outcasts and think only good concerning them."

Olam Ha Beriah/Interindividual stage Ones can be idealistic reformers whose principled, uncondescending stands lead them to fight for truth and justice. Thus, Cordevero writes:

> He should always seek mercy and blessings for all creatures.
>
> He ought to petition constantly for their deliverance from oppression ...
>
> He will think of those who are cut off, seek out the needs of the young, heal those that are broken; feed the needy and return the strayed ones ... let him not hold himself aloof or find such tasks debasing; but let him lead as each requires to be led.

For Cordevero, the result of these actions is to bring the Ones not only to good conduct but to a unique identification with *Chochmah* which will help restore its proper influence upon the divine and our world. "He will be led ... into Righteousness in Upper Thought (*Chochmah*) which guides *Adam Kadmon* aright." (This is the *sefirot* configured as Primordial Man. See Chapter 2 for more details.)

7

Point Two:
Binah—Understanding

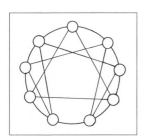

OF THE VARIOUS ENNEAGRAM types, Twos are deemed to be the **Caregivers**. Having lost their connection to the Holy Idea of **Will**, the sense that their needs will be met naturally, through the purposeful unfolding of life without having to manipulate or serve others, Twos have learned that to receive you must give. They develop a mental fixation of **Flattery**, which they use to charm other people. They also develop the emotional passion of **Pride**, which makes them feel indispensable to those whom they help. Instinctually, the Two's Subtypes are aggressively **Seductive** in intimate situations; **Ambitious** to secure the attention and prestige of being associated with powerful people in social situations; they feel that, because they give so much, they have the right to a "**Me First**" privilege in the preserving of their own well-being.

It is not coincidental that the *sefirah* that correlates to the Two is *Binah*. This *sefirah* embodies understanding, which is a core trait of the Two. Twos can intuitively sense the special needs of others and offer them just the help they require. Just as its corresponding aspect of Essence, Holy Will, represents the universal intelligence that guides the unfolding of reality with purpose and direction, so too does *Binah* guide the succeeding seven *sefirot* of the *Etz Chayim,* allotting to each that aspect of *Shefa* (radiant energy) it needs to manifest its own unique divine trait.

PERSONALITY AND ITS TRAITS

Motivated by a need to be needed, Twos tend to be loving and supportive. Desiring both physical and emotional closeness, Twos can remain strongly committed to relationships in which they feel wanted. Appearing altruistic to a fault, they can give great amounts of their time and energy to others. "No" is a hard word for a Two to say. In groups, Twos make everyone feel welcome, aid others in their tasks and are sensitive to how shared decisions effect everyone involved.

However, this seeming selflessness can mask an assumption that others can accomplish nothing without their indispensable aid. When their efforts go unrecognized and their love unreturned, Twos can become vindictive and move from portraying themselves as saviors to acting first as victims and then as persecutors. Underlying the giving nature of the Two is a certain manipulative dynamic. If love and security can be gained by meeting the needs of others, then the Two will do this. Control can be achieved by being helpful and making themselves indispensable—and then pointing out how much others are indebted to them. Twos describe this manipulation in this way:

> "I'm the one who can help. I'm indispensable. It's a prideful stance, manipulative and invasive." "I have a real sense that only I can do it. This is a compulsion to

help others, and thereby, to get my own needs met indirectly."

Often, Twos will attach themselves to powerful people so they can bask in the reflected glory of being invaluable to those with undeniable status. Such people have the power and influence to ensure that the Twos' desires are met. While growing up, Twos were loved when they pleased others. As such, their sense of worth developed in response to how others reacted to them. They learned to adapt their personality to fit the desires of others and to read others' emotional states through their smiles, frowns, gestures and expressions. But being so other-directed made them lose touch with their own needs. They wonder if they are really loving or playing a role of how a loving person should act. Tensions can develop between the Two's desire to merge with his or her partner and a strong conflicting desire to break free.

Twos can be quite flirtatious and seek sexual attention as a sign of approval. But even more than sex, they want to know that they're wanted even if they aren't sure that they want the object of their flirtations. Twos are most energized when moving toward challenging relationships, being attracted to attached partners not to hurt the partner's spouse, but to overcome the hurdle of that partner's unavailability. True intimacy, however, can threaten the Two because it might expose the fact that there is no real self inside them.

The qualities of the Two at the *Tsadik* level emerge as empathy and sincerity; a deep commitment to help others without thinking of personal gain; and compassion and forgiveness. At the *Benoni* level these characteristics manifest as over-friendliness and flattery; cloying codependence in their need to be needed; imposition of themselves on others so as not to be abandoned; and playing the martyr to prove their own worth. *Rashah* level traits can appear manipulative, histrionic, and self-serving; they can instill guilt in others. *Rashah* Twos may act as custodians of others in order to bind people to them; they may abuse people, food, and substances to mask feelings of being unappreciated.

ASCENDING THROUGH THE *OLAMOT*

At the Conformist/*Olam Ha'asiyah* stage, Twos seem completely other-directed. Often they feel unsure of their inner emotions and who they really are, so they constantly adapt to meet the expectations of others. To elicit love they suppress their own feelings and make others' agendas their own. Fearing rejection, they control others through helpfulness, feeling anger when not receiving the appreciation or emotional response they seek. They try to achieve status by identification, if not actual association, with the prestigious and powerful. Seeking attention and approval, they may focus on externals, doing what the "right" people do and adopting the fashions they wear. They usually keep their circles of acquaintance separate, so they can avoid having to meet potentially conflicting expectations at the same time.

At some point in their lives, the role of constant caregiver may become stifling for Twos. The *shevirah,* or break, that pushes them forward might occur due to betrayal or by becoming overwhelmed. Wanting to be free, they begin to look inside and claim their feelings of anger and anxiety over constantly seeking others' approval. Entering the Conscientious/*Olam Ha Yetsirah* stage, they begin to question who they really are, identify their own ideals, and let go of the ideals of others with which they have falsely identified. They begin to interrupt their shape-shifting patterns and start to discern when help is truly needed and when it is intrusive. By gaining clarity about their own feelings, they can become more objective about the feelings of others and set the stage for real rather than feigned intimacy. Instead of projecting their feelings onto others or changing themselves in the search for affirmation, this greater personal authenticity can help engender the mutuality needed for real love. Adjustments might be needed at this stage. The previously overburdened Two might be tempted to throw off any responsibility for others, to move from co-dependence to independence. Those whom the Two previously nurtured may apply both subtle and overt pressure because they want their dependable caregiver back.

Those Twos who enter *Olam Ha Beriah,* the Interindividual stage, find their worldview expanded. No longer keeping their circles of acquaintances separate and acting differently with different groups, they now use their adaptive skills positively to network and break down barriers among people. They are able to live with the polarity of wanting attachment to others and wanting to be free, with the paradox that self-care is part of caring for the world and growing closer to oneself allows for truer communion with others. Able to recognize the difference between needed help and manipulative control, they can clarify their reasons for supporting given issues or causes, and give magnanimously without counting the benefits or the costs. Helping others actuate their own potential, particularly those of low status who can offer no reward, is now experienced as a privilege in the fullness and depth of the Two's being.

THE BIBLICAL HEROINE: *IMA*

Whether male or female, Twos are often noted for their mothering qualities. Their pride mimics their lost Essence of Holly Will, which spurs them to think they can willfully satisfy all needs. At the *Olam Ha'asiyah*/Conformist stage, Twos can be possessive and smothering. Functioning at the higher stages, Twos become genuinely nurturing enablers. Kabbalists have personified the corresponding *sefirah, Binah,* as the Supernal Mother, *Ima.* If *Chochmah* is portrayed as a seed, then *Binah* is the womb into which the seed is implanted. All individualization takes place therein and ultimately all the other seven *sefirot* emerge from *Ima.*

Like the Two, in fixation, there is a controlling aspect

to *Ima*. As the Well or Fountain of Blessing, it is *Ima* who continues to nourish and sustain each of her sefirotic off-spring even after they have emerged from her. Just as the Two offers different aspects of his or her personality to different people, so does *Ima* mediate her divine energy through different paths to each *sefirah*.

While maintaining an attachment to the other *sefirot*, *Ima* looks forward to the time of *Hitball'ut*, Cosmic Reintegration, when her *sefirotic* children will return to her. However, rather than shackling or smothering them, that return will be the ultimate Sabbath and Jubilee. Like the *Olam Ha Beriah*/Interindividual Two, *Ima* will then enable each *sefirah* to go out to freedom and ascend to its own essential higher state as part of *Ayn Sof*.

SHA'AR/GATEWAY

In *Pirke Avot*, the *Ethics of the Fathers*, deeds of loving kindness are listed with worship and Torah study as one of three pillars upon which the world stands.

Each morning, at the very beginning of the synagogue liturgy, worshippers recite a list of these loving acts, which are known in Hebrew as *Gemilut Hasadim*. They include providing hospitality to travelers, visiting the sick, ensuring that the indigent have the means to marry and showing proper respect to the deceased both by attending funerals and by consoling the bereaved. These deeds are considered so important that those who perform them are rewarded in this world and throughout eternity.

Given the Two's inclination toward helpfulness, these activities might provide an appropriate starting point for their Jewish involvement and spiritual growth. Working with committees that help comfort the bereaved and assisting the ill and the needy seems a natural way for Twos to use their talents and find a place within the Jewish community.

Through prayer and study of sacred texts, Twos and others can learn that these loving acts are more than good deeds or ways to gain self-validation through helpfulness.

Judaism actually views them as ways of imitating God. Scripture bids us to "walk after God" and Israel's sages tell us the way to do that is "to be compassionate as God is compassionate." Reciting prayers each day like Psalms 145 and 146 remind us that God's dreams for the world include feeding the hungry and helping those who are vulnerable and dispossessed. By performing these and other loving acts, we become partners in making God's dreams become real.

TIKKUN/REPAIR

Afflicted with the Passion of pride, Twos need to develop the virtue of Humility as a path back to Essence. To do so, Cordevero recommends in *Tomer Devorah* the spiritual discipline of *Teshuvah,* or Repentance:

> How should one train in the quality of *Binah*?
> By Repentance, for there is nothing so worthy ...
> *Binah* tempers judgments and destroys their bitterness
> ... return in true penitence and correct every imperfection.

At first glance, it would appear strange that a caring, giving Two would need to repent. Yet each of the three stages of repentance can be beneficial to the Two.

The first step, *Vidui,* is that of confession. Rather than inflate one's importance to others or exhibit false modesty, the Two needs to recognize and admit his real worth and his own real needs. This confronting of who one is without the false tendencies of self-exaltation or debasement is the beginning of real humility. This can also lead to admitting that manipulation and control can often be the motive behind the Twos' helpfulness. In this way, Twos can move toward the higher qualities of their security point, Four, and begin to recognize their own true emotions and needs.

Tefillah, or prayer, is the second stage of repentance. For those who see all help emanating from them, prayer can be beneficial in asking for divine assistance and in cultivating humility. Not only can prayer provide insight, but it can disabuse Twos of the illusion that everyone needs them while they don't need anyone.

The final act of Repentance is performing loving, charitable deeds. These are known as *tsedakah,* whose root is *tsedek* (righteousness). *Tikkun* can be achieved if one now offers care and nurture without counting the benefits or costs, without seeking ways to control others or for self-validation, but simply because the cause is right. Cordevero wrote:

> If you do well you can root yourself in the mystery of repentance, converting formerly evil deeds to their root in the mystery of the good ... accusers ... are converted into good sponsors.... Thus one cleanses the harmful inclination (*Yetser HaRa*), brings it into the region of the beneficial (*Yetser Ha Tov*), and replants him in holiness.

The literal meaning of the Hebrew word for repentance, *teshuvah,* is "return." This is the same word used to describe the ultimate return of the seven succeeding *sefirot* to *Binah.* Perhaps the lesson for Twos is that cloying and control will not prevent others from abandoning you. Only by freely giving care can you ensure that others will want to return in friendship to you. And through repentance, the redeemed Two can hasten *Hitball'ut* (the time of Cosmic Reintegration into Essence). As Cordevero writes, "Whoever lives all his days with thoughts of repentance causes understanding (*Binah*) to shine upon all his days ... and the days of his life are crowned."

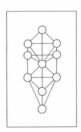

8

Point Three:
Gedulah—Greatness

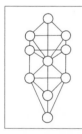 THREES HAVE BEEN ALTERNATIVELY called **Succeeders, Achievers** or **Performers**. Having lost the Essential state of **Hope** that good things can occur, independent of their efforts, Threes learn to gain approval through achievement. Preoccupied with the fixation of **Vanity** in maintaining a winning **Image**, the Threes' passion for **Deceit** can lead to "polishing" defeats and portraying themselves as more accomplished or prestigious than they really are. Instinctually, Threes who are in intimate relationships strive to present themselves to their partners as embodying the ideal **Image** of a male and female, pursue **Prestige** and status in social groups and seek material **Security** as a sign of self-worth in the area of self-preservation.

Gedulah, or greatness, is the *sefirah* which corresponds to Point Three. Like Hope, its corresponding Holy

Idea, *Gedulah* is the abundant, flowing grace of divine energy and love. Portrayed in the imagery of *Adam Kadmon,* *Gedulah* is God's strong right arm.

PERSONALITY AND ITS TRAITS

Threes occupy the core point of the Enneagram's feeling or heart triad. Twos want to be loved by others. Fours want to be understood by others. Threes want to be admired by others.

If Threes have a motto, it is "You are what you produce." Having been prized for what they achieved, Threes compete well for personal victory or to rally their team. Threes can become the exemplars of the highest ideals of those groups they deem significant. As masters of promotion, Threes can move directly from an idea into action. Using activity as a way to avoid depression, they keep full schedules and always have several balls in the air.

Because appearing successful is of ultimate importance to them, Threes fool themselves and others about how successful or how busy they really are. They may abandon faltering projects before a failure occurs or blame can be assigned. Authenticity and depth can be sacrificed for superficiality as long as the status is high, the title is right and the check has enough zeroes.

There is a chameleonlike quality about Threes that lets them change their personae to fit the ideal of each group with which they are involved. Experts at advancing themselves, Threes are vain about their importance to a project. Concerned with personal status, they play to win and seek positions of authority and power over others.

Threes describe their approach to image and competition this way:

> "Image needs to be present all the time, whether it's appearing as a corporate executive, a biker or as a member of the society horse set. It seems like I'm doing what I need to do and I'm not really practicing a

form of deceit." "I'm going to win. If I don't, I'll rationalize that I've won some way."

Threes prefer to associate with those who are accomplished and attractive and usually remain close to others
only when they are engaged in a project or social activity.
When romantically involved, Threes may project the
image of an ideal, sensitive lover while expressing feelings
that don't really correspond to their true emotions. During
a moment of great intimacy, their attention may shift else-
where.

The qualities of the Three at the *Tsadik* level emerge
as energy, resourcefulness, self-assurance, infectious en-
thusiasm, and an unqualified commitment to support the
worthy goals and projects of others. At the *Benoni* level
these traits manifest as being driven and preoccupied
with success, projecting whatever image will gain the
most admiration, social climbing, and being competitive to
the point of disparaging others. At the *Rashah* level, Three
characteristics appear as vanity, hollowness, pretentious-
ness, a mortal fear of failure, and the willingness to lie,
cheat, and betray others to maintain their self-image.

ASCENDING THROUGH THE *OLAMOT*
For Threes at the Conformist/*Olam Ha'asiyah* stage the
truth is whatever works and produces results. As indicated above, success is gauged by meeting measurable
standards and goals, both in achievement and reward.
While Twos alter themselves to meet the expectations of
significant individuals, Threes shape-shift to embody the
ideals of whatever group is important to them at the
moment. They so appropriate the group's energies and
priorities that they actually feel the feelings of the roles
they are playing. As long as acclaim is forthcoming and a
winning image is maintained, why worry about the real
self? Since outbreaks of emotion are messy and detract

from productivity, it is easier to play the role of a lover or one bereaved than it is to actually feel the feelings.

Perhaps due to illness, perhaps due to failure despite best efforts and competence, the Three can begin to realize a difference between achieving the external signs of success and real personal well-being. This shattering of identification with accomplishment and the group can enlarge the Three's perspective in the deeper search for who she really is. This process of creating an authentic self-identity can be painful: Remove the roles and the masks and what is left? If I am not feeling the role's feelings, how am I supposed to feel?

As the Conscientious/*Olam Ha Yetsirah* stage unfolds, the Three will become more willing to pause before moving into action; more willing to ponder, to consider, to wait. There is a greater desire to align his actions with how he is really feeling than with group expectations or what will achieve results. Self-promotion may now feel embarrassing. His relationships can deepen as he is no longer relating role to role, but he may experience different feelings with and from different people. The possibility of greater empathy and emotional loyalty emerges as concern for others eclipses the Three's instinctual concern for how others are responding to him. At this stage the Three may trade the overt mask of acquisitiveness and status-seeking for a more refined mask. Rather than strive for authenticity, he might assume a sensitive, thoughtful, or spiritual persona, depending on the traits valued by the groups that he now identifies with.

At the *Olam Ha Beriah*/Interindividual stage the Three becomes increasingly more able to articulate her feelings and to accept vulnerability and failure. She can live in the dynamic tension of her need for both intimacy and achievement, with her desire for leadership and for self-care. No longer enslaved to the reaction of others, she lives with greater tranquility, her outer life more reflective of her inner principles and goals. Mutuality and interdependence now mark her enlarged range of personal relationships. Efficiency now includes being true to herself and a fuller awareness of the contexts in which she can make real contributions to the world. Now able to collaborate, she can share the stage with others, take pleasure in their successes, and unselfishly, even anonymously, promote the good of the group. Her natural energy combined with a heightened sense of loyalty can mobilize others at times of reversal and inject new hope when faced with despair.

THE BIBLICAL HERO: ABRAHAM

Kabbalists have viewed the biblical figure of Abraham as the incarnation of *Gedulah*. The tales about Abraham reveal that he exhibited characteristics of the higher and the lower *Olamot*/Stages of the Three. Although the Torah tells nothing of Abraham's childhood, rabbinic lore indicates that great achievements were expected from him even before his birth.

God lured Abraham to his mission with three promises: Abraham would become a mighty nation, he would receive material blessings, and he would achieve a great reputation. Obviously, God knew Abraham well because the possibility of success, prosperity and a grand image spurred Abraham to leave Mesopotamia for Canaan. Fearing that he might be killed so that someone else could take his wife, Abraham twice falsely introduced Sarah as his sister, once to Pharaoh (Genesis 12:13) and once to the Philistine King Avimelech (Genesis 20:2). The result of each charade was the enrichment of Abraham's family.

An effective, forceful leader, Abraham formed a successful alliance following the defeat and enslavement of Sodom by the King of Elam, Chedarlaomer. Abraham freed the captives, including his own nephew, Lot. Yet even at his altruistic best, when he refused personal gain from his victory, Abraham exhibited a lingering concern with image, declaring, "Let no one say 'I have enriched Abraham'" (Genesis 14:23).

Despite these foibles, there were moments when Abraham became the paradigm of the human ideal and the best a person could be. When confronted with the impending destruction of Sodom, Abraham argued with God that the righteous might be killed unfairly with the wicked (Genesis 18:25). Before concluding a political alliance with Avimelech, Abraham delayed negotiations until the Philistine ruler clarified a matter of stolen wells even though Abraham himself might not have been among the injured parties (Genesis 21:25). Even in the midst of his most terrifying mission, the abortive sacrifice of Isaac at Mount Moriah, Abraham was able to say three times *"Hineni,* I am here and fully present"—in response to God, to his child Isaac and finally to the angelic call which bade him to refrain from harm and stay his hand (Genesis 22). And finally, despite his image as a mighty prince of God, Abraham personally attended to the details of Sarah's funeral by purchasing her burial plot at an exorbitant fee, eulogizing her, weeping openly and burying her with his own hands (Genesis 23). For these reasons, the prophet Isaiah considered this *Olam Ha Beriah/* Interindividual Abraham worthy of the title "God's Friend."

SHA'AR/GATEWAY

Although Judaism has a rich philosophic tradition, its greatest emphasis is on action. This orientation is summed up by the previously quoted statement that it is not the exposition but the deed which is essential. Rather than having long lists of dogmas, Judaism is centered around performing *mitzvot,* divine commandments that prescribe how every aspect of our lives can be sanctified by specific acts. These range from worship to the observance of dietary laws to business ethics.

This pragmatic approach should prove appealing to Threes who are at the beginning of their spiritual journeys, and who are not inclined toward ongoing introspection. The realization that God can be served by concrete acts that have practical rationale can provide Threes with a comfortable entrée into the Jewish quest for spiritual life. The idea of being validated by what you *do* corresponds to the orientation of the Three.

Within Jewish life, there are ample opportunities for those, like Threes, who wish to assume leadership roles. From congregational committees and boards to leading services and reading scripture to involvement in charitable and Zionist enterprises, there are numerous chances to step forward, do needed work and receive recognition. However, the Hebrew terms for doing community work, *Tsorchai Tsibbur,* and leading in worship, *Shaliach Tsibbur,* literally mean meeting the "needs of the community" and being the "messenger of the community." Both phrases alert Threes and everyone else that such godly work is not for personal aggrandizement, but for the common good.

TIKKUN/REPAIR

The virtue of the Threes is *Honesty.* For those at more advanced stages of the journey, Cordevero's *Tomer Devorah* recommends immersion in the love of God. This leads away from the unceasing pursuit of status, worldly gain, and a winning image, and provides a transcendent constancy:

> The main entry ... is by way of utter love of the Lord which he will not desert for any cause ... it behooves one to first arrange for the needs of divine worship and ... [then] look to his other needs. The love of God should be fixed in his heart regardless of whether he receives bounty or suffering.

In the Bible, the foreskin represented whatever obstructs our true generative powers. It metaphorically blocks truth and God's word from penetrating our heart. Drawing on this imagery, Cordevero instructs that:

> ... every action must be performed properly ... and every semblance of husk or foreskin must be removed.

> Every cause which produced this foreskin must be
> pursued ... in such a manner ... he cuts away the fore-
> skin from his own heart causing the righteous to be
> without husk.

Rather than social climbing and appearing only in the company of the attractive and the accomplished, Corde-vero prescribes performing the following acts to be a human paradigm: visiting and healing the sick, giving donations to the poor, providing hospitality for the homeless, dowering indigent brides and making peace with others. These acts come naturally for Twos and can be their entry point into Judaism. For Threes, they serve a different purpose. They highlight the *Chesed* of *Gedulah,* the dedicated kindness inherent in true greatness, and move Threes toward the *Olam Ha Beriah*/Interindividual qualities of loyalty and commitment to others devoid of self-promotion.

When performed with *kavannah* (proper intention) the disciplines described above not only assure the Threes' real attainments in this world, they trigger cosmic ramifications as well. By acting kindly, by taking responsibility for one's defeats and setbacks in life, and by trying to derive lessons about personal goodness from them, Threes can balance *Din*'s limitations, which is located on the Left side of the *Etz Chayim* with the kind fullness of the Right side's *Chesed.* These acts can strengthen the proper alignment of *Tiferet, Yesod,* and *Malchut* along the Center pathways, bringing the flow of *Ayn Sof's* light to the spheres below.

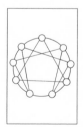

9

Point Four: Tiferet—Beauty

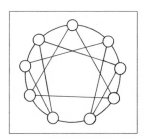 FOURS, WHO ARE CONSIDERED the most self-aware of the Enneagram types, have been labeled **Romantics**. Constantly feeling that something vital is missing from their lives, Fours were wounded in their Essence of **Origin**. They are convinced that somehow they were abandoned from an ideal, original state in which all things were deeply and fully connected. Because they long for what is no longer there, Fours develop a Fixation of **Melancholy**, the sweet sadness of yearning, and the Passion of **Envy**, the jealously that others are being fulfilled while they are not. On the instinctual Subtype level, Fours **Compete** with a rival for a desirable mate as a sign of self-worth in intimate situations. They might feel **Shame** for not meeting group expectations in social settings, and prove **Reckless** in taking risks because "living on the edge"

provides them with the emotional exhilaration they need to preserve an authentic sense of themselves.

The parallel *sefirah* on the *Etz Chayim* is *Tiferet,* the *sefirah* of Beauty. Like Origin, its corresponding Holy Idea, *Tiferet* is the locus of interconnection, the *sefirah* that links all of the *sefirot* together. Just as Fours are always perched between the alternating flatness of what is available and the attractiveness of what is distant, *Tiferet* is caught between its neighboring *sefirot* in an ever-shifting, precarious position of balancing the expansive grace of *Chesed* and the limiting judgments of *Din.* Just as human lovers are described as "soul mates," so Kabbalists describe *Tiferet* and *Shechinah* as *du parzufin,* "twin faces" of each other. Because *Shechinah* is now separated from the *Etz Chayim,* because of Adam and Eve's fall, *Tiferet* longs for reunion with its lost love and forms the heart of a configuration of six *sefirot,* which is called *Zeir Anpin,* the Impatient, Yearning One.

PERSONALITY AND ITS TRAITS

Quite unlike any other type, Fours can sense the pulse and emotional tone of a room. For them, mood plays as much a part in making decisions as objective data; the implications and the feeling of a conversation can be more important than the words exchanged. Fours' sensitivity can lead them to creativity in art, drama, music, and literature. Fours are energized by life's key moments—birth, marriage, illness, death—and don't cave in when crises occur.

Fours jealously wonder if others are enjoying rewards or emotional satisfaction that are being denied them. Having sensed abandonment early on, Fours focus on feelings of deprivation. Rarely living in the present, which is too mundane and flawed, Fours alternate between yearning for romanticized moments from the past when all seemed right and an inaccessible future when all will be perfect. Fours describe their envy and yearning in the following way:

"It's not so much that someone has what I don't. It's more that they're something that I'm not because I'm deficient."

"Why don't I have what they have? I'm just as special as they are."

"It's not what we've got now which is important. It's what we once had."

"You can get lost in the reverie of your imagination."

Fours' preoccupation with class and beauty is an attempt to embroider the drabness of the present and to boost their own self-image from being an abandoned pariah to being a unique outsider with a distinct flair. Needing to stand apart from the crowd, Fours may flout convention by courting scandal.

Eschewing what can be obtained in favor of what no longer is or what does not even exist, Fours exhibit Melancholy, a regret for what has been lost sweetened by the hope of possible fulfillment in the future. Frequently descending into depression, Fours can react to their sadness by hyperactivity or artistic expression, by wild shifts in mood, or by succumbing to despair and suicidal urges. Because they feel that they have been deserted because of their own unworthiness, Fours can turn abandonment into a self-fulfilling prophecy and sabotage relationships by focusing on others' imperfections.

"Does he really love me? I'm not sure I'm worthy. I feel fear and deep hurt when my partner withdraws. I just want to cry my eyes out."

"I fear that they'll find out that I'm deficient and abandon me. Therefore, I create situations which force them to leave and then say, '*You're* the one who is abandoning me.'"

Qualities of the Four at the *Tsadik* level emerge as creativity, self-awareness, gentleness, compassionate empathy for another's pain, and the ability to inspire others in their search for authentic individuality. At the *Benoni* level these Four characteristics manifest as artistic romanticism, melancholy, hypersensitivity, self-pity, and self-exemption from the standards that govern others. At the *Rashah* level, Four traits appear as self-destruction, depression, alienation, torment, and a focus on the negative in themselves and others.

ASCENDING THROUGH THE *OLAMOT*

Conformist/*Olam Ha'asiyah* Fours live in a world of flair and emotion, driven by the desire to connect, to feel fulfilled. Out of touch with any inner feelings of contentment they seek fulfillment through externals, yearning for an absent friend or lover, for material goods, or status to mark them as special. Not realizing that it is personal wholeness they seek, they are inevitably disappointed when the desired relationship or acquisition is achieved and still they feel unfulfilled. As detailed above, this dynamic leads to valuing what is absent, disparaging what is present, and envying others not for what they have, but because their perceived sense of fulfillment highlights the Four's unhappiness. Mood swings are commonplace and melancholy, the sweet sadness of separation and longing, forms the backdrop of their lives. Feeling abandoned and alienated, they often grow impatient with this mundane world and can be quite critical of others and themselves.

Over the course of time the weight of continual yearning and melancholy, of feeling different and alone, can become too heavy for the Four to bear. Growing more introspective, he can come to realize how his penchant for drama and flair has been feeding his fixations of envy and melancholy, how he has actually drawn his identity from alienation and yearning.

Becoming more self-aware at the Conscientious/*Olam Ha Yetsirah* stage, the Four may recognize the dynamics that underlie his outbreaks of emotion and assess their consequences. Discovering ongoing areas of satisfaction in his life can help him to examine his melancholy and even allow him to use it purposefully as a tool of compassion, sensing others' sorrows. Grace and originality now replace exaggeration and flamboyance as the Four's inner sense of self seeks authentic outer expression. Able to experience a whole range of emotions, he more realistically looks at the positive and negative present in all relationships. While able to experience greater intimacy at this time, the Four must be careful not to give way to previous fears of abandonment by precipitous actions or outbursts of drama that can subvert the very connections he is trying to engender.

Having harmonized their inner sense of authenticity with their outer behavior, Interindividual/*Olam Ha Beriah* Fours now live with greater equanimity and are more self-reflective. Satisfaction is now found in actual life rather than in yearning for unfulfilled dreams; they can even detect and bring subtle beauty into ugly situations. Willing to risk hurt to stay present in intimate connections, their relationships reflect greater mutuality and the ability to enjoy life's blessings in the moment. Seeing others as works of art, these Fours use their gifts of sensitivity to help others beautify their own lives. Possessing a high level of authenticity and empathy, they can both detect that which is false and companion others through painful experiences. Their vision of the possibilities for the renewal of this world in all its beauty can make them dauntless in their pursuit of filling in that which is incomplete in life.

THE BIBLICAL HERO: JACOB

Kabbalists portray the third Jewish patriarch, Jacob, as the embodiment of *Tiferet*. Like *Olam Ha'asiyah*/Conformist Fours, Jacob seemed to grasp for what lay beyond his reach. Attempting even before birth to be the elder of a set of twins, he enviously snatched at his brother Esau's heel as they left Rebecca's womb (Genesis 25:26). In his latter years, Jacob was discontent, even melancholy. Having just been reunited in Egypt with his beloved son, Joseph, Jacob still told the Pharaoh, "The years of my sojourn are one hundred and thirty, few and bad, not having yet attained the years of my fathers" (Genesis 47:9).

Not above playing at the edge of scandal, Jacob cheated Esau first of his birthright (Genesis 25:29–34) and then of their father's blessing (Genesis 27). While living in Mesopotamia, Jacob again skirted authority by secretly devising a way to augment his own flocks when he felt cheated by his uncle Laban (Genesis 30:28–43).

Originally described as a mild man (Genesis 25:27), Jacob was later given to great passion. Arriving in Haran as a fugitive from Esau's wrath, he weepingly hugged and kissed his cousin Rachel even before they were properly introduced (Geneses 29:11). In typical tragic-romantic fashion, Jacob longed for Rachel when she was inaccessible. He worked seven years and then another seven years so they could marry (Genesis 29:28–28). Once they were wed, however, he scoffed at her despair over her infertility (Genesis 30:1 & 2). When she died while they were on a journey, Jacob didn't even take a half-day's trip to the family plot in Hebron. Instead, he buried Rachel on the way to Bethlehem (Genesis 35:19). Only long after she died did Jacob again express his yearning for her, giving his sons the impression that only Rachel, rather than Leah or the handmaidens, was his truly beloved wife (Genesis 44:27).

Jacob's great moment of uplift came upon returning from Haran to Canaan. Anxious about confronting his brother Esau, who was accompanied by armed soldiers, Jacob wrestled with the angel of his real fears and emotions, refusing to let go. Although he was wounded in his struggle, he achieved the status of *Israel*, "Champion of God," because he had "striven with God and men and prevailed." In an act of true sensitivity, Jacob made restitution for the hurt he caused by taking Esau's blessing. Offering Esau a large gift of servants and domestic animals, he implored, "Please take my blessing which I have brought for you." When Esau demurred, Jacob beseeched him to accept. Although the less prosperous of the two, Jacob, with rare equanimity, told Esau, "I have everything" (Genesis 33:11).

During his last days, Jacob, in *Olam Ha Beriah/* Interindividual Four fashion, gave each of his sons an authentic evaluation of their respective characters to help them enhance their lives. Judah and Joseph were praised; Reuben, Simon, and Levi were chastised and told how they should improve. During these final exchanges with his sons, Jacob asked that he not be buried amid the opulence of Egypt, but with his ancestors in Canaan.

SHA'AR/GATEWAY

Hiddur mitzvah is the principle that impels us to go beyond a perfunctory observance of Judaism. Literally, the term means to "adorn the commandments." By using decoration and beautiful ritual objects, we enhance our own aesthetic appreciation of Judaism while demonstrating that God and God's commandments are precious to us.

Given their artistic nature, Fours can find a special path to serving God through *hiddur mitzvah*. Each Friday night, the Sabbath table can be spread with a lovely cloth and adorned with flowers and beautiful place settings, with special chalices for *Kiddush* (the blessing over the wine) and an embroidered cover for the braided loaves of bread (*challah*). Each festive occasion can be marked as special through its own unique ritual objects; a beautiful *menorah* (candelabrum) for Hanukkah; a silver or finely glazed seder plate for Passover; an artistically lettered and decorated *Ketubah* (marriage contract) for a wedding. These items can be purchased or hand-crafted according to personal taste and inclination. The choice of dress, the physical ambience of the setting and even the melodies used to sing the prayers can all help point beyond personal adornment toward the beauty of observance.

Memory and yearning play integral roles within Jewish life. *Zachor,* "remember," commands us to recount how God redeemed our Israelite ancestors from Egyptian bondage, to recall martyrs from the past and to remember our own loved ones who have gone before us. Even the High Holy Days are referred to as Days of Remembrance. The mournful strains of the prayer, *Ani Maamin,* tell of how we believe fully in the coming of the Messiah and how we will wait and yearn even though that moment of arrival seems forever delayed.

Jewish tradition can teach *Olam Ha'asiyah*/Conformist Fours and others that memory and yearning should inform and inspire us rather than paralyze and depress us. Examining our own deeds or our own people's history can provide us with springboards to further growth and the faith that renewal can come after tragedy strikes. Anticipating an era of Messianic goodness and peace can encourage us to hasten that era by using each moment to make the world more compassionate and just.

Tikkun/Repair

Given the Fours' penchant for self-absorption, Cordevero counsels in *Tomer Devorah:*

> How should one train himself in the quality of beauty?
> There is no doubt ... study the Torah.

For Fours who are given to subjective thinking and skirting the rules, studying Torah can move them toward the higher qualities of their Security Point, One, by indicating that there are, indeed, objective standards and values. Caught in their shifting moods and their ambivalent struggle with intimacy, the Torah can help teach Fours that rules of action call us beyond our emotional responses, that there are obligatory ways we are expected to treat others. Rather than yielding to despair, Fours can take heart from the archetype of redemptive love that is displayed through Israel's redemption from Egypt.

Fours who are preoccupied with being classy and desiring to associate with the "right people" can, by studying Torah, be led to see the sanctity in helping the downtrodden. As Cordevero writes in *Tomer Devorah:*

> When man treats the poor with proper consideration beauty will shine.... It behooves man to mix freely with all creatures and be considerate of all men.... It becomes the wise to deal gently with them ... never lord it over those designated as "dust of the earth."

If envy caused by attraction to the unavailable is the Fours' Passion, then *Equanimity* in feeling satisfied with one's situation is their Virtue. Humility in seeking a true sense of God through Torah can help achieve such a balance. It can temper the judgmental with a sense of grace and lead us to *Olam Ha Beriah*/Interindividual appreciation of the miraculous which can be found in the everyday. Discussions about the Torah undertaken in the name of Heaven can lead to peace and end in love.

When one studies and teaches Torah without desire for self-aggrandizement, *Tikkun* also occurs on the Cosmic level. Engaging in Torah "for the sake of Heaven" helps balance *Chesed* and *Din* (kindness and stricture) while shining *Tiferet* (divine beauty) upon *Yesod* and *Malchut* to our world below.

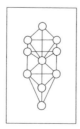

10

Point Five: Din—Rigor

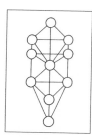 FIVES ARE LIFE'S **OBSERVERS**. EXPE-
riencing the world as a demanding place
with scant rewards, Fives have lost the Holy
Idea of **Omniscience**, of directly connecting
to the world so they can know it as it essen-
tially is. Hence, Fives acquire knowledge and
protect their personal space by minimizing
contact with others and simplifying their own needs. More
comfortable with thinking than with feeling, Fives develop
a mental Fixation of **Stinginess** and an emotional Passion
of **Avarice** as they hoard information, time and privacy
and guard themselves against outside intrusion. On the instinctual Subtype level, Fives can exchange **Confidences**
and bond privately with another in an intimate situation.
In social situations, they create their own niche by offering
their group specialized expertise or archiving the group's
history as if they were guarding a sacred **Totem**. To

preserve themselves, they establish **Castles,** personal safe havens from outer intrusion.

Din (rigor) is the *sefirah* that corresponds to the Five. If *Gedulah* is expansive grace, then *Din* is stricture and containment. Like Omniscience, its corresponding Holy Idea, *Din* emphasizes differentiation and discrimination within the cosmic whole. Seen as God's left arm, *Din* cordons off, compartmentalizes and sets boundaries. It provides the exacting judgments that relegate everything to its own proper place.

PERSONALITY AND ITS TRAITS

Fives, who are contemplative people, have a unique ability to grasp ideas, theorize, and make abstract or obscure information relevant. Uncomfortable with broad social contacts, Fives prefer solitude. They find it energizing and it gives them the privacy to process their real feelings and revel in personal fantasy. Fives would rather make do with less than become entangled with the emotional demands of others. Having experienced either abandonment by loved ones or a psychologically intrusive family, Fives survive by detaching themselves from their emotions and are perceived as cold, aloof and self-protective. Even when appearing in public, Fives hide behind a pose so they can avoid real involvement.

Fives seem trapped by a sense of emptiness, as if they have a hole inside that can never be filled. Emotionally stingy, they are uncomfortable with the word "share" and are not natural parents. They like predictability so they can preview situations before they occur. They keep friends and interests compartmentalized so emotionally charged experiences don't flow into each other. By mastering grand concepts such as psychology or sociology, and then by locating their own place within these systems, Fives try to understand people and events without having to experience them emotionally.

Faced with either confrontation or intimacy, Fives disengage from their feelings to render themselves emotionally immune or to figure out where they stand. Following this, Fives might make a mental commitment to a personal relationship before committing themselves emotionally to it. Sometimes they find greater ease in intimacy through nonverbal sexual expression. While being able to offer advice, analysis or counsel to those around them, Fives do not easily commiserate about feelings.

One Five described himself this way:

> "I'm a learner who is searching for a unifying principle to life."
>
> "I've meditated now for twenty-five years."
>
> "As a technical problem solver I make my living through thinking and I read, study and write for my own satisfaction."
>
> "I feel agitated and anxious in groups. My room is my castle where I can be alone with my computer."
>
> "Sometimes when I write, I get stuck trying to finish it, but for me the process is more important than the completion."
>
> "I know I have a ways to go in developing personal skills and empathy, but I'm idealistic and love to grow."

Qualities of the Five at the *Tsadik* level emerge as profundity, subtlety, and the ability to detect patterns that otherwise would go unnoticed. At the *Benoni* level these characteristics manifest as the replacement of feeling with thinking, demanding large amounts of privacy, and overanalyzing of details born out of the fear that the Five will never know enough.

Five traits at the *Rashah* level appear as disconnection from reality, miserliness, rejecting social contact, and withdrawing into a world of their own mental constructs because ordinary life seems dangerous.

ASCENDING THROUGH THE *OLAMOT*

At the Conformist/*Olam Ha'asiyah* stage, Fives find the external world fearful, filled with meddling, intrusive people. Their real world is mental and private, one in which they think through things without often communicating them to others. They might be aware of their feelings; beneath the surface, Fives' emotions may even run deep within them. Detached from these emotions, however, Fives have a hard time differentiating their feelings from their thoughts. They observe others, observe themselves, and observe themselves observing others. Virtual modalities like the Internet allow them to be in contact without actual contact, and if they join any groups at all they seek specialized interest groups. In addition to their privacy, acquiring the external symbols of knowledge, including academic degrees, a large personal library, and personal connection to recognized experts in their chosen fields can be very important to them. Their thirst for knowledge may be born of their desire to understand themselves. However, their fear of being exposed or overwhelmed impels them to remain hidden through scarcity, noninvolvement, and emotional control.

At some point, feelings of love or anger that the Five wanted to keep hidden may erupt. She may be faced with the loss of a relationship she found significant, even though she might not have communicated her feelings to the other. This can lead to a realization that commitment, with all its spontaneity, intimacy, and stress, might actually constitute personal gain rather than loss.

Arriving at the Conscientious/*Olam Ha Yetsirah* stage, this Five is now less willing to hide, more aware of her inner desires, and better able to engage her feelings. More transparent, she is less likely to flee from passion and is willing to risk exposure with someone who really loves her. While stilled controlled on the inside, she feels better able to outwardly hold her ground and can experience the rush of power that comes with acknowledging justifiable anger. Open to a greater range of options and activities, this Five appears more outgoing. While noninvolvement can still be a deliberate choice if needed, she now feels freer in public, more generous, less concerned with others' credentials, and more inclusive in her relationships. While better able to express her feelings, it is still a challenge to the Five at this stage to move toward others rather than waiting for others to move toward her.

At the Interindividual/*Olam Ha Beriah* stage, Fives are more comfortable in their own skin and better able to balance their desires for both privacy and intimacy. Their observer style now becomes a tool to achieve greater understanding of their inner feelings, of their responses in relationship, and of the areas in which they need further growth. Their ability to achieve emotional distance can now be used consciously to gain perspective, offer accurate evaluation, and bring calm to turbulent, charged situations. More sensitive to the feelings and priorities of others, they can be warm, supportive confidants who work quietly to help others actualize their own goals. Their own intellectual searching, and their encouragement of others to join in that search, can bring authenticity and quality to their social groups and the world beyond.

THE BIBLICAL HERO: ISAAC

The *sefirah* of *Din* is identified with the patriarch Isaac. Seen by his aged parents as the divine fulfillment of their long-awaited dream, Isaac was raised in an emotionally intrusive environment. His parents threw a huge party on the day he was weaned. His mother, Sarah, who was very protective, banished his half-brother Ishmael for mocking Isaac (Genesis 21:9–10). This sense of intrusion must have been multiplied exponentially when Isaac found himself almost slaughtered by Abraham at Mount Moriah, where he was literally bound to the altar of his father's beliefs (Genesis 22). So great was Isaac's detachment from the world after his near-sacrifice that the Bible does not mention that he attended his mother's funeral, nor does it offer any details about the next three years of his life.

Like an *Olam Ha'asiyah*/Conformist Five seeking to avoid entanglements and confrontation, Isaac moved from Philistia to Rehoboth to Beer Sheba before finally standing up to the aggressiveness of the Philistines and their king, Avimelech. He did not remonstrate his son, Esau, even though he was troubled by Esau's marriage to two pagan women (Genesis 26:13–35). This lack of involvement was never more evident than when he let Rebecca and Jacob claim Esau's blessings through a ruse that led to enmity and the breakup of their family (Genesis 27). Various commentators claim that Isaac's blindness was not only a physical impairment of old age. Figuratively, it was manifest when he let his sons grow up almost on their own (Genesis 25:27).

At his *Olam Ha Beriah*/Interindividual best, Isaac was a contemplative man with great insights. He dug deeply, finding wellsprings and fountains that had gone untapped since the days of his father Abraham (Genesis 24:18). He was given to meditation in the field (Genesis 24:63), and Jewish tradition credits him with composing the afternoon *Minchah* service. When Rebecca faced infertility, Isaac prayed on her behalf so they could have children together. While expressing neither compliments nor yearnings for his wife, as Abraham had for Sarah and later Jacob would have for Rachel, Isaac shared a joyous nonverbal intimacy with Rebecca, often frolicking with her (Genesis 26:8).

Perhaps because he had been separated from his brother, Ishmael, and later faced his own death while being bound on the altar, Isaac developed a deep knowing quality. He recognized the true characters of his twin sons, but knew that life was too short for fighting. Perhaps this is why he was willing to give Esau the blessing usually reserved for the firstborn even though he disapproved of Esau's lifestyle (Genesis 26–34). His hope was that if one son had the material blessing and the other son had the spiritual birthright, they could live together in harmony. When this proved untenable, he gave the special spiritual blessing of Abraham to Jacob, who Isaac felt would cherish it more than would the earthy Esau, before Jacob fled to Haran to escape Esau's wrath.

A beautiful rabbinic homily indicates that at the end of time, the fate of the People of Israel will hang in the balance. Perhaps dismayed by their offspring's misdeeds, Abraham and Jacob will concur with God and let their descendents be condemned for their sins. However, it will be the insights and pleas of the more reserved Isaac which will save his children from damnation. And his many sons and daughters will leave the abyss of judgment, declaring, "Isaac, our true father is you."

SHA'AR/GATEWAY

Study is considered to be among the most important of all Jewish virtues. Indeed, some consider it to be the prime *mitzvah* and many Orthodox Jewish communities are organized with their *Yeshivah,* (Talmudic academy) as the central communal institution. Statements like *"v'Talmud Torah k'neged kulam"* literally mean that Torah study is equal to all other religious and charitable activity.

For Fives and all others who like to study, Judaism considers education to be a lifelong adventure. If one wishes to investigate grand conceptual systems, there is the world of *Halachah* (Jewish law) which includes texts from the Talmud to contemporary legal responsa and covers every aspect of human existence. One can learn the Bible and its commentaries, the philosophical writings of Maimonides and other great thinkers or explore the mystical framework of Kabbalah.

Judaism holds that study, *Talmud Torah,* is more than a cognitive activity. It should move *Olam Ha'asiyah* Fives and other learners to study with others, to teach, and to act upon what has been learned. Study is also meant to emotionally transform the lives of those who learn. This is illustrated by the tale of a student who told the Kotzker Rebbe, a nineteenth-century Hasidic rabbi, that he had been through the whole Talmud ten times. "Very nice," replied the Kotzker, "but how many times has the Talmud been through you?"

Tikkun/Repair

The *sefirah* of *Din* is also known as *Gevurah,* which is "might" or "heroism." This name suggests that Fives, by moving toward the higher qualities of their Security Point Eight, should become more forthright. Rather than remaining reclusive and uninvolved, Fives need to move toward the higher *Olamot*/Stages by using their knowledge and insight courageously to help and lead others. Thus, they can become true heroes, not only by aiding those around them, but by overcoming their own inclinations to withdraw.

In *Tomer Devorah,* Cordevero counsels that we should begin emotional engagement through the love of a spouse. To the detached, he writes

> ... For your mate's sake arouse your passions gently, providing clothing and suitable dwelling.... From this point of view one may arouse passion by the love of a spouse.... This should provide the approach to all manner of passion ... employ them primarily to your partner whom God has determined for you.

Fives often disengage from life for fear of involvement, seeking the privacy of a safe refuge. They hoard their time and ego resources lest intrusions deplete them. The Fives' Virtue is *Non-Attachment,* which differs from detachment. It is being able to experience a full range of feelings without being compulsive about any one emotion, about treasuring what is valuable without being overly possessive.

In moving Fives toward intimacy, Cordevero counsels

non-attached engagement that comes not from the passion of sexual arousal "nor desire for gain nor anger nor the pursuit of honor." Rather than retreating to a "castle," the *Olam Ha Beriah*/Interindividual Five's home can be a beautifully adorned place of sharing.

Such nonattached engagement can have redemptive cosmic implications. It balances the stricture of *Din* with the sweetness of kind *Chesed* and keeps the destructive passions in check. The resulting intimacy with one's mate mirrors and hastens the union of *Shechinah* with the rest of *Adam Kadmon* and leads to God's grace flowing to the world.

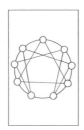

11

Point Six: Netsach— The Enduring

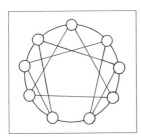

SIXES ARE KNOWN EITHER AS **Loyal Skeptics** or **Devil's Advocates**. Seeing the world as a threatening place, Sixes have been wounded in their essential state of **Faith** in themselves and others. Always surveying the environment for signals of danger, Sixes develop a mental fixation of **Cowardice** and an emotional passion for **Doubt and Fear**. Phobic Sixes respond to their fear by flight or by seeking the safety of groups; the Counter-Phobic Six will run headlong into dangerous situations to make what is fearful go away. On an instinctual Subtype level, Sixes will play to their **Strength and Beauty** as ways to counter their fears of intimate situations, ensure the loyalty of their group by adhering with **Duty** to its social rules, and in the area of self-preservation, use personal **Warmth** to disarm the harmful intent of others.

The *sefirah* that correlates to the Six is *Netsach*. This translates as "eternity," or that which endures. Like Faith, its corresponding Holy Idea, *Netsach* ensures perseverance even in the face of despair. Given Sixes' search for safety in tradition and authority, their loyalty to relationships over the long term and their ability to see extended tasks through to the end, *Netsach* is the potency of the Six.

PERSONALITY AND ITS TRAITS

Sixes are the adhesive that holds society together. Motivated by honor and duty, they create and maintain organizations and are concerned with the well-being of the community. Dependable and giving of themselves, Sixes are alert to threats and will defend the weak and the vulnerable. Faithful to their commitments, Sixes are secure in groups with people who have been proven trustworthy.

Point Six occupies the center slot of the Enneagram's head triad. Its Passion, *Fear,* is born not of emotion but by always thinking, "What *if* this or what *if* that?" While Fives deal with fear through detachment and Sevens try to paint a smiling face over it, Sixes assuage their fear by appealing to the practices of tradition, the dictates of a leader or some other outside authority. Because many Sixes were raised in unpredictable environments, they lost faith in their own power to act and in the trustworthiness of those in control. This explains their identification with traditions and power beyond themselves—and their healthy dose of cynicism. While seeking a strong leader, Sixes will also be suspicious of the leader's intentions.

Sixes function well in a defined hierarchy, work against odds without recognition and remain loyal to the group under pressure. However, their tendency to procrastinate can undermine their success because they fear that public prominence will invite hostile attack. Sometimes they place themselves in urgent situations that eliminate the time they need to think before reacting.

Wary of being seduced by praise, they constantly

scan the landscape for hostile intentions and might angrily attribute their own unworthy desires to others. At times, they envision the worst without bothering to also envision the best. Sixes are loyal spouses given to long-term marriages, but, they take a long time to trust their mates. They often wonder whether their partners praise them only to seek personal advantage or whether courtship might be a prelude to desertion.

Sixes describe their orientation in this way:

"I used to catastrophize, What if this or what if that? all the time. All I had to do was get on a plane and I'd imagine the worst happening. Once a jet we were on had a problem. My husband handled it wonderfully, but not me."

"... [Life is full] of treacherous situations. You need to constantly scan the environment to prepare for pitfalls."

"I've been in a relationship for eight years and I still fear, 'Does he really love me? Why doesn't he do this or let me do that?'"

Qualities of the Six at the *Tsadik* level emerge as warmth, hard work, cooperation, loyalty, and the courage to champion the underdog. At the *Benoni* level these traits emerge as anxious sociability, support for groups and causes as a way to avoid making personal decisions, and either the idolization or undue suspicion of those in power. *Rashah* Six characteristics manifest as ripe dependence, self-disparagement, and constantly seeking direction from others. If Counter-Phobic, these traits include bullying the weak, persecuting "inferiors," hate-mongering, and projecting their own sense of inadequacy onto scapegoats. Both can fall prey to those offering simplistic answers to complex problems.

ASCENDING THROUGH THE *OLAMOT*

At the Conformist/*Olam Ha'asiyah* stage, fear forms the backdrop of Sixes' lives. Whether Phobic or Counter-Phobic, they constantly scan the environment looking for hidden motivations and lurking danger. Imagining the worst, they project their inner fears outward, looking for the holes in every argument and the biases that influence the context of each discussion. Finding introspection diffi-cult, they judge others on the basis of external norms and behaviors; prone to being authoritarian, they see things as right or wrong, black or white. However, their relation-ship to authority is wrought with ambivalence. On the one hand, their doubting minds always question the com-petence and trustworthiness of the leader; on the other, there is stability and security to be found in authority, so they will often take on the philosophy and behavior of their chosen groups as a means of assuring their own safety.

Approaching the Conscientious/*Olam Ha Yetsirah* stage, Sixes may begin to turn their doubting minds to-ward the laws and group regulations to which they have subscribed. They may also sense conflict between loyalty to the group and their ties to individuals important to them. Growing more reflective, their thinking becomes less stereotypic, more flexible, and better able to entertain the validity of multiple possibilities. Excessive group loy-alty lessens as they become more open to deepening inter-personal relationships. Sensing the consequences of their fear driven fixations, they begin to work at dispelling those fears and achieving greater tranquility. At this stage they may still feel frightened and vulnerable when facing their inner desires and still fear the dangers that might lurk beneath even justifiable pleasures.

Able to clearly distinguish between reality and the pro-jection of their own fears, Interindividual/*Olam Ha Beriah* Sixes exhibit both self-confidence and comfort in the pres-ence of others. Able to live with greater ambiguity, they evince the bravery to be independent and interdependent, to formulate and pursue their own paths. Their doubting minds now become moving forces for truth and clarity, unearthing wrongs that might be invisible to others. Intuitive readers of others and themselves, they now find hidden resources in others to advance their growth, supporting and challenging them simultaneously. Knowing the debilitating nature of doubt, they look compassionately on the hesitancies of others and are willing to sacrifice themselves on their behalf. With a sense of loyalty and duty that extends beyond those nearest to them, they are able to confront evil, champion the downtrodden, and help advance the cause of humanity.

THE BIBLICAL HERO: MOSES
The biblical character Kabbalists deemed to be *Netsach* incarnate was Moses. Exhibiting loyalty and an ability to work long and hard, often with little satisfaction, Moses left the palace of Egypt to work as a shepherd in Midian for his father-in-law, Jethro. Later, Moses gave up the security of Midian to return to Egypt and lead a band of less than grateful former slaves through the wilderness for forty years.

From infancy, Moses learned that the world could be a fearful place. To save him from the execution that awaited all Israelite baby boys, his mother sailed him down the Nile in a basket when he was three months old (Exodus 2). We can imagine that young Moses, growing up as the adoptive son of Pharaoh's daughter, was constantly scanning his palace home for signs that his Hebrew background was in danger of being exposed. While his ability to intuit the hidden intentions of others was needed to redeem and lead the Israelites from Pharaoh's bondage, Moses, like the *Olam Ha'asiyah*/Conformist Six, perceived threats at times when there was no threat. Once he inaccurately suspected the Israelites of wanting to stone him (Exodus 17:4); he later wrongly accused the tribes of Reuben and Gad of attempting to divert their fellow Israelites from entering Canaan (Numbers 32:1–15).

At different times, Moses displayed qualities of the Counter-Phobic and the Phobic Six. Championing the underdog even early in his career, Moses smote an Egyptian taskmaster who was beating a Hebrew slave. Later, he rushed into danger and single-handedly beat back Midianite shepherds who were abusing Jethro's daughter. Not exempt, however, from procrastinating when exposed to the spotlight or to pressure, Moses marshaled every imaginable argument to forestall accepting God's mission as Israel's redeemer (Exodus 3, 4:1–17). During the wandering in the wilderness, Moses twice vacillated when his hungry people demanded meat (Numbers 11) and later thirsted for water (Numbers 20).

The greatness of Moses was that, at eighty years of age, his sense of duty and loyalty to his heritage led him to return to the Pharaoh's court so that he could eventually lead an unruly pack of former slaves across a treacherous wilderness. His sense of obligation and obedience moved him beyond the highest stages, making him worthy to become the medium through which God's traditions and imperatives were transmitted to future generations.

SHA'AR/GATEWAY

Sixes at the *Olam Ha'asiyah*/Conformist stage seem to have two conflicting tendencies: the need to question and the desire for security. Judaism is a religion that can provide both answers and security.

An old joke maintains that Jews answer questions with other questions. While this is not always the case, our tradition of inquiry goes back to Abraham. It was he who questioned God's motives for destroying Sodom with the words, "Shall the Judge of the whole world not act justly?" (Genesis 18:25). The grand corpus of classical rabbinic law, the Talmud, is arranged as a series of questions and answers which lead to even further debate and response.

Each year at our Passover seders, we encourage our children to ask the Four Questions, beginning with "Why is this night different from all other nights?"

Jewish tradition encourages informed inquiry and feels that only at the End of Days, when the prophet Elijah will return to herald the Messiah, will all outstanding issues be resolved.

While questioning is an important Jewish activity, Jews are not left to face life's uncertainties without guidance. Jewish tradition and practice provide us with familiar signposts on the path of life. From welcoming newborns to bidding our deceased farewell, the wisdom of past generations and the support of our communities can help Sixes, and all Jews, develop a sense of trust and security, even when life seems chaotic.

Tikkun/Repair

In response to fear, *Courage* is the Virtue of the Six. This courage is not the absence of caution, but the ability to respond to challenges and danger appropriately. Moses exhibited courage by overcoming fears about his age, his speech impediment and whether he was still a wanted man in Egypt. He did all this so that he could free an enslaved people.

Given Sixes' loyalist tendency to idolize the strong leader and desire to impose simple answers on complex matters, Cordevero recommends the following in *Tomer Devorah:*

> ... Scripture says, "From all my teachers have I received understanding (Psalms 119:99)"; for mastery cannot be achieved when received but from one master. Whoever becomes a disciple of all merits becoming a chariot ... "the instructed of the Lord" (Isaiah 54:13).

This receptivity to a variety of opinions can help lead Sixes toward the higher qualities of their Security Point, the open, receptive Nine.

To counter Sixes' vulnerability to the appeals of hate groups and to abusing the weak, Cordevero suggests that they dedicate themselves to such worthwhile causes as helping those who study God's ways:

> As a first step assist the students of Torah and assure their support ... that they may proceed with their studies undisturbed. Never disparage ... honor them and praise good deeds ... care for the procurement of necessary books, for the maintenance of the House of Study ... [through] support by word of mouth, personal service, financial support and arousing the interest of others.

Not only should Sixes assist those who study Torah but, teaches Cordevero, "When he reads Scripture ... he has a personal relation to *Netsach*." Such study leads toward the *Olam Ha Beriah*/Interindividual stage by engendering an understanding of right action and a truer ability to evaluate the worthiness of others' world views. Learning Scripture can also help restore Sixes' lost Essence of Faith because it teaches about God's redemptive love, which gives us a sense of security in this dangerous world.

According to Cordevero, studying Scripture has sublime ramifications. It helps to realign the center pathways of the *Etz Chayim* and brings the divine radiance from *Tiferet* through *Netsach* to the world below.

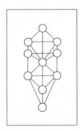

12

Point Seven:
Hod—*Splendor*

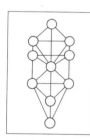 SEVENS, THE MOST UPBEAT OF ALL PER-
sonality types, are known as **Adventurers**
and **Epicures**. Frustrated in the Holy Idea of
Plan, that one can actualize the full realm of
life by progressing purposefully from one
stage to another, Sevens use their imaginations to flee from pain and seek pleasure.
Rather than deal with a fearful present, Sevens develop
their own mental Fixation of **Planning** an endless variety
of exciting future alternatives. To ward off boredom,
Sevens' emotional Passion, **Gluttony**, seeks to feed their
vast hunger for stimulating and enjoyable experiences. On
the Subtype instinctual level, the Sevens' imaginations
make them:

- *Suggestible* to sharing a realm of fascinating
  options with a partner in intimate situations;

- Willing to endure temporary limitations and *Sacrifice* to achieve a brighter future in social settings;

- Surround themselves with the security of *Like-Minded Defenders,* who reflect back to the Seven his or her own life view. This ensures a sense of personal well-being.

On an Essential level *Hod,* like its corresponding Holy Idea, Plan, represents the actualization of the Universal Design underlying all of reality in its specific details. When preoccupied with self, however, Sevens can only see the world as a reflecting pond of their own splendor, the arena to actualize their own glorious plans. At the levels of both Essence and personality the *sefirah* of Splendor, *Hod,* corresponds to Point Seven.

PERSONALITY AND ITS TRAITS

Sevens are generally optimistic. Usually blessed with a variety of skills and interests, Sevens can work endlessly and handle several jobs at one time. Easily enthused about new enterprises, Sevens keep group morale up and are innovative because they can intuit connections between seemingly unrelated options. Disliking confrontation and accusations, which might impugn their worth, Sevens quickly replace the negative with more promising possibilities.

In many ways, Sevens and Threes resemble each other. Both are optimistic, competitive, and seek the praise of others. Where Threes seek their value in earned achievement and the pursuit of power, Sevens see their worth deriving from their own inherent value and might strive for status as one of a number of interesting things on the agenda. Buoyant and energizing, Sevens constantly anticipate a glorious future and believe in the limitless possibilities of life.

Retaining only wonderful memories of their youth, Sevens mentally recast even painful events. By using their imagination to embroider life, they deny its dark side and block hurtful memory. Possessing a Pan-like, eternal child quality, Sevens have an idealized self-image. Uncomfortable with recrimination because it implies that they are flawed, Sevens just move on to the next task on their agenda. A packed schedule leaves little time for self-examination.

Sevens love to be admired by interesting people. Using charm as their stock in trade, they'll talk their way out of trouble. They consider no one to be above them and they adopt egalitarian stances to hide their basic anti-authoritarian posture of "you can do it your way as long as you let me do it mine." While enthusiastic about new tasks and able to synthesize novel approaches, Sevens might lose interest in the middle of a project as its scope narrows and becomes "old."

As with work, Sevens can be innovative with relationships. Finding emotionally dependent people difficult to bear, they desire to be close to those who love adventure and a good time. Not only do Sevens want a whole range of activities within their relationships, they also seek the freedom to maintain a wide scope of interest outside the relationship. If a partner nurses a hurt for too long, the Seven will leave in search of more upbeat relationships. One Seven described her approach to life in this manner:

"I consider myself fun-loving, happy and accomplished. If it wasn't for my positive attitude, I don't think I would have made it through the recent tragedies in my life. My perfect day would have forty-eight hours. The first twenty-four would deal with sales and all the things I want to do professionally. Then I'd need another twenty-four to play tennis and party and be with friends ... I don't deal well with heavy emotions. I like people like myself: upbeat, successful and interesting."

Qualities of the Seven at the *Tsadik* level emerge as life-affirming joy, energy, resilience in the face of loss, optimism, and a willingness to sacrifice personal advantage for a better group future. At the *Benoni* level these Seven characteristics manifest as self-absorption, a continual search for wider experience to keep boredom at bay, seductive charm, flight from pain, and a discomfort with limits. *Rashah* Seven traits appear as superficial narcissism; depression; rage when denied their desires; addiction to food, alcohol, or substances; and a near infantile evasion of responsibility.

ASCENDING THROUGH THE *OLAMOT*
At the Conformist/*Olam Ha'asiyah* stage, Sevens fear that life is restrictive, that present reality is both inhibiting and boring. They seek to cover that fear with humor, activity, and the continual pondering of alternatives, possibilities, and creative ideas. To avoid the pain that often comes with deep emotions, they replace feelings with fantasies; these need not all be realized but provide the illusion of freedom through the potential of endless options. Another Seven hedge against fear is to make lots of like-minded friends with whom to share plans and adventures. In their narcissistic use of the group to gain recognition and appreciation, they often over-estimate their ability to move and inspire others. Their innate sense of entitlement leads them to think that by right they can circumvent authority and, if not, their charm will extricate them from sticky situations. Defeats will inevitably be reframed as partial victories, learning experiences, or someone else's fault.

At some point Sevens may run up against painful experiences they cannot rationalize away. They begin to realize that others may not share their preferences, their way of thinking, or what they find amusing. Arriving at the Conscientious/*Olam Ha Yetsirah* stage, they become more self-reflective and self-dependent. They start to question previously held assumptions, such as pleasure is always good and guilt is always bad. Pain now can be recognized as a catalyst to personal growth, guilt a tool to discern right from wrong. Uniqueness can be claimed by committing to a single path rather than jumping between multiple options. Rather than acting like takers who will flee at the slightest hint of boredom or pain, these Sevens feel they have something deeper to give and are more willing to remain present through the inevitable disappointments and suffering that relationships bring. The challenge at this stage is maintaining personal commitment by recognizing that a relationship's true importance lies in its quality and not merely in its ability to provide fun.

Better able to differentiate their inner life from the outer world, Interindividual/*Olam Ha Beriah* Sevens can now discern the difference between fantasy and actual pleasure. Cognizant of the reality of limits, they can find fresh potentialities within those limits, bring their ideas to fruition, and maintain interest throughout the entire process. Willing to struggle with the demands of intimacy, they can remain open to the possibilities that can come even from negative experience and interactions. More socially aware, they find pleasure in helping others and are able to see the consequences of seemingly trivial choices that can lead to injustice. Rather than merely exploring options, they are able to synthesize diverse information and use their propensity for planning to envision and help actualize a better world. Consciously subordinating their own needs to those of the group, they can energize others, which helps Sevens keep their dreams alive.

THE BIBLICAL HERO: AARON

Kabbalists view the High Priest Aaron as the embodiment of *Hod*. Despite the effects of enslavement upon the Hebrews, the Torah does not mention that Aaron had bad memories about his youth. Perhaps his buoyancy and sense of specialness came from the fact that the Levites, Aaron's tribe, were spared from slavery so that they could minister spiritually to the other Israelites. This could only have been bolstered by his serving first as Moses's prophet and then as the High Priest.

As a man who moved from one activity to the next, Aaron sought to lighten the spirits of the Hebrew slaves. He went back and forth between the court and the slave camps, helping Moses gain Israel's freedom and then helping him lead the Exodus. As High Priest, he moved in glittering vestments from animal sacrifices to lighting incense to reconciling disputes to annulling misdirected vows. Aaron's flurry of action left him little time for reflection or family.

Like many *Olam Ha'asiyah*/Conformist Sevens, Aaron was unable to see the dark side of life. His optimism and ability to synthesize seemingly irreconcilable options made him legendary as an arbitrator and peacemaker among feuding spouses and friends. However, when a mob pressed him to make a Golden Calf, Aaron accommodated them, not realizing the tragedy and the alienation from God he was unleashing (Exodus 32). His own activities kept him from seeing the destructive path of his two elder sons, a path that included substance abuse, disobedience to God, insensitivity to women and arrogance toward elders. When his sons died during their day of priestly ordination, Aaron was struck mute (Leviticus 10).

Perhaps Aaron's highest attribution was his attainment of *Olam Ha Beriah*/Interindividual life-affirming resilience in the face of this personal horror. After the death of his sons, Nadav and Abihu, Aaron donned special vestments and entered the Holy of Holies to seek atonement for the people Israel on the first Yom Kippur. Rather than seeking infantile escape from his miscalculation regarding the Golden Calf and his bereavement over his sons, Aaron was sensitive to the needs of others and acted as the medium for their reconciliation with God. Because of his enthusiastic, conciliatory optimism, all Israel mourned Aaron's passing, a tribute not even afforded to the stricter Moses.

SHA'AR/GATEWAY

Psalm 100 states, "Serve the Lord with gladness; come before Him with singing." This call to sacred joy is known as *simchah shel mitzvah,* literally the "happiness that attends performing God's will." Sevens and others can discover a true sense of celebration in many aspects of Jewish life.

Shabbat is a time to join in festive meals, to sing and dance and share in the beautiful gift of the Sabbath. The Feast of Booths, Sukkot, is called *Z'man Simchateynu,* "the Season of our Joy." During each of the seven days of Sukkot, we parade through the synagogue with citrons and raised palm branches (*etrog* and *lulav*) and praise God's saving power. At the conclusion of the festival, we rejoice during *Simchat Torah* by reading the end of Deuteronomy and the beginning of Genesis and by dancing fervently through the sanctuary with the Torah scrolls. On Purim, the Feast of Lots, we don masks, rattle noise makers and drink to celebrate Mordechai and Esther's triumph over the anti-Semitic Haman in ancient Persia. Passover, the "Season of our Liberation," is enjoyed with loved ones at the beautiful seder meal, when we eat, drink four cups of wine, recount our ancestors' enslavement and sing of redemption. Births, bar and bat mitzvah and marriage all have their own life-passage celebrations.

These moments of sacred joy can direct *Olam Ha'asiyah*

Sevens, and us all, to look beyond mere revelry toward greater Jewish spiritual commitment. On these days, we express our gratitude for the blessings God has showered upon us and rededicate ourselves to doing God's will.

TIKKUN/REPAIR

Always flitting about, Sevens crave action and new experiences to avoid any painful realizations that might come from reflection. Seeking the fresh and the novel, Sevens can lose interest in tasks that have become stale and quickly move on to new adventures.

In *Tomer Devorah,* Cordevero tells how Sevens can move toward the higher *Olamot*/Stages and achieve their Virtue of *Sobriety.* Sixes were called upon to support worthy institutions, not those that mock others or generate animosity. Sevens should also join in that task as their way to promote perseverance and commitment:

> ... assure their [the students] support, either by financial contributions or by actual deeds such as supplying them with the necessaries—that is, with food—or satisfying any other of their wants ... the more one honors the Torah by personal service ... the more one becomes rooted and fixed.

The Security Point for Sevens is Five, the point of reflection detached from acquisitiveness. To achieve the higher reflective qualities of Fives, Cordevero suggests that Sevens should study *Mishnah* (the primary Talmudic codification of rabbinic law). Because Sevens are prone to excess, this exploration can teach that life's wondrous possibilities are to be sanctified, but not hedonistically devoured. Such study can reveal the gap between self-centered, arbitrary behavior and a way of life which has ongoing sacred obligations and which pulses with a divine rhythm. Perhaps this will help Sevens face the pain and self-questioning that they habitually avoid.

Hod is the *sefirah* envisioned as the left leg of *Adam Kadmon.* By studying *Mishnah,* Sevens help to strengthen *Hod* so that it, together with the right leg, *Netsach,* can properly support the other *sefirot.*

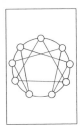

13

Point Eight:
Yesod—Basic Force

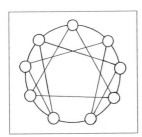 IF ONES ARE GOOD AND OBEDI-
ent, then Eights are bossy **Confron-
ters**. They are life's "bad girls and
boys." Wounded by a harsh world in
which the strong unjustly try to impose their "truth" upon the weak,
Eights have lost a sense that a univer-
sal **Truth** applies to all individuals. To correct injustice,
Eights mentally fixate on **Vengeance**; to hide vulnerability
and avoid boredom they develop the passion of **Lust** to acquire power, control and the intensity that comes from excess. On the instinctual Subtype level, Eights first move
toward **Possession**, toward controlling the heart and
mind of their partners before they are willing to be vulnerable and surrender themselves to those they love. Eights
seek **Friendship** with people who will stand up to them
and remain steadfast in social relations while seeking to

control their personal environment to achieve **Satisfactory Survival** in matters of personal well-being.

Yesod is the *sefirah* which parallels Point Eight on the Enneagram. Like Truth, its corresponding Holy Idea, *Yesod's* function in the *Etz Chayim* is to constitute all the energetic dimensions of the *sefirot* into an inclusive unity. Translated as "base" or "foundation," *Yesod* functions as the male reproductive organ of *Adam Kadmon*. In its phallic symbolism, *Yesod* is the channel for the outpouring of masculine generative force. The potency of *Yesod* is also known as *Tsadik*, indicating that, employed righteously, power can be a foundation of existence.

PERSONALITY AND ITS TRAITS

Combative by nature, Eights learn at an early age that the strong are respected and the weak are not. Therefore, they feel secure only when they call the shots and will use whatever leverage they have to win. Able to struggle against great odds, Eights show their love by offering protection to others. Always on the lookout for those who have power and whether they will be fair, Eights can seize control of a situation to avenge injustice.

Because they view the world as hostile, Eights are preoccupied with maintaining control over anything that can influence their lives. They only develop trust when others act without hidden agendas. Confrontational, they intuitively hone in on others' weak spots to see if they'll crumble, stand by their positions or retaliate. They are willing to polarize social situations through controversy to expose others as honest or false, friend or foe. Eights focus on breaking down others' defenses, leaving no room for alternative rationales or self-blame. Fully energized by conflict, Eights would rather fight a worthy opponent than score an easy win. Rather than admit defeat, Eights will bear grudges and plan how they will ultimately triumph when they meet their foe again.

Never cowering no matter what the obstacle, Eights

always consider themselves more powerful than their opponents and will fight through injury, blocking out physical and emotional pain. Disdaining those who avoid conflict, Eights see themselves exempt from strictures that bind weaker people. In effect, they want to make rules for others—and then flout those rules themselves. Eights only become hesitant when torn between exposing their own tender feelings and denying them. Their more caring side comes into play when called upon to protect the small or the weak or when they feel they can trust another person enough to risk vulnerability.

Having had their childhood innocence stolen by adversity, Eights instinctively look outward for someone or something to blame. Therefore, they are largely free from self-recrimination and self-reflection. Unembarrassed by their anger, their appetites, or their libido, Eights will overindulge in whatever makes them feel good and powerful, including food, sex, drugs, drink, or work. Basically loners with low frustration levels, Eights might create conflicts with others just because they're bored by the lack of a real challenge. Eights describe themselves in the following way:

> "I grew up in a hostile environment with lots of random violence. I just had to get tough. Justice seemed tied up with revenge."
>
> "From the outside, my actions might look like vengeance. But inside, its like correcting a wrong, like redressing the balance."
>
> "When I face someone weak or vulnerable, my soft, feminine feelings stir up."
>
> "Too much of a good thing is almost enough."

Qualities of the Eight at the *Tsadik* level emerge as assertiveness, leadership, moral and physical courage in the face of overwhelming odds, and the tendency to protect the outcast and the weak. At the *Benoni* level these same characteristics manifest as formidability, dominance, antagonism, and contempt for those who "can't take it." Eight traits at the *Rashah* level appear as ruthlessness, megalomania, exploiting the weaknesses in others, and the desire to humiliate and degrade them.

ASCENDING THROUGH THE *OLAMOT*

At the Conformist/*Olam Ha'asiyah* stage, Eights seem to take over, to fill up all the space in the situations they find themselves. Impervious to other points of view, they see only black and white based on surface impressions and are sure that their brand of truth and justice is what the world needs. While maintaining that others should follow the rules, they are more than willing to personally set them aside to pursue what they perceive as a higher good. Eights constantly test others for signs of resistance or submission and will focus their laser-like attention on any sensed weaknesses. Driven and defensive, they will dismiss unconscious feelings and conflicting evidence to vanquish their foes and will justify their aggressive feelings and behavior as being necessary to right wrongs.

Faced with limits on their ability to impose their version of justice on the world or the realization that others may have valid reasons for holding differing opinions, Eights begin to arrive at the Conscientious/*Olam Ha Yetsirah* stage. More tolerant of contradiction and exceptions, life now takes on shades of gray, and inner feelings reveal nuance that goes beyond anger and oppositional reactivity. Recognizing the consequences of their anger upon others and themselves, they begin to move away from false absolutes toward a broader, more objective view of justice. Better able to control their impulses, having internalized behavioral standards, they can now open to their softer feelings and allow their natural goodness and honesty to come through. Mutuality of interest, trust, and generosity begin to replace conflict and control as these Eights deepen and broaden their relational styles. A challenge for Eights at this level will be their discomfort at living with uncertainty and a desire to reclaim the absolutist clarity that previously energized them.

Now able to balance their needs for achievement and intimacy, for independence and dependence, Interindividual/ *Olam Ha Beriah* Eights show greater tolerance for ambiguity and the willingness to connect with others just as they are with no need to dominate them. Their broader perspective helps them realize that self-fulfillment can come from uniting with others, that we are all responsible for the state of the world, and there is no need to be punitive. Less defensive, they are willing to find freedom in dependence on others, to risk surrendering to intimacy and mutuality in love. Their previous drive for control and excess is here transformed into a commitment to promote the welfare of others. Feeling safe themselves, their concern and protection help others feel safe.

THE BIBLICAL HERO: JOSEPH

Because he shunned Mrs. Potiphar's advances and remained sexually chaste (Genesis 39:7–10), Kabbalists designated Joseph as the ideal biblical incarnation of the *Sefirah Yesod,* pictured as the phallus of *Adam Kadmon.* A closer examination of Joseph's life indicates that, although not physically violent, he did exhibit higher and lower characteristics of the classic Eight.

Experiencing early adversity, Joseph lost his mother at a young age (Genesis 35:16–20). Joseph was the eleventh of twelve sons, and his brothers were a rough lot who attacked the city of *Shechem* to avenge the seduction of their sister Dinah (Genesis 34). They hated Joseph because he was their father's favorite son. Sensing their greatest vulnerability, Joseph told them about two dreams that indicated they would bow down to him (Genesis 37:5–11). They responded by throwing him into a pit and selling him to a caravan of Ishmaelite traders headed for Egypt.

Joseph also exhibited an *Olam Ha'asiyah*/Conformist

talent for verbal probing and attack while in Egypt. He used sarcasm when interpreting the dreams of Pharaoh's chief butler and baker with whom he was in jail following the incident with Mrs. Potiphar: "Pharaoh will lift up your head ... then he will behead you" (Genesis 40:12, 19). Later, as viceroy of Egypt, Joseph enacted a plan by which surplus food was stored during seven years of plenty and then distributed during the following seven years of famine. When Joseph's brothers came to Egypt from Canaan looking for supplies, they didn't recognize him. He used his powers first to imprison Simon and later to threaten Benjamin to test the brothers: would they now be loyal to each other, or would they abandon another brother as they had abandoned him? When Joseph revealed his true identity to his brothers, he again skillfully inserted his verbal knife. Responding to their concern for the elderly Jacob's life if Benjamin were imprisoned, Joseph asked, "Is my father still alive?" This was a rebuke to them for not showing concern for their father when they had sold Joseph.

No matter what the situation, Joseph seemed to take control of it. Even in his youth, he considered himself more powerful than his brothers. Rising from slave to foreman in Potiphar's home, from convict to trustee in prison and finally from prisoner to viceroy in Pharaoh's court, Joseph always ended up in charge. A decisive leader, he was able to formulate a plan and mobilize all Egypt to overcome a seven-year famine.

In true Eight fashion, Joseph became concerned when he again confronted his brothers. Should he let himself be vulnerable to sympathy toward his family or should he deny his feelings? He then set in motion a whole series of tests to see if his brothers would stand true to each other or crumble. It was only after Judah offered his own freedom as a ransom for the younger Benjamin that Joseph felt he could trust the brothers and open up emotionally to them (Genesis 44, 45:1–8).

Having moved toward the *Olam Ha Beriah/* Interindividual stage, the mature Joseph proved a true champion of the endangered. His method of food distribution during Egypt's lean years provided food for all while thwarting black marketeers. The brash boy who dreamed of growing up to control his siblings finally realized not to use his power for self-aggrandizement, but to help the weak and hungry.

SHA'AR/GATEWAY

God's call to imitate God's ways extends beyond showing compassion to the needy. It also includes protecting the weak and the downtrodden, causes that naturally appeal to Eights. Psalm 146 proclaims, "The Lord guards the stranger. The Lord upholds the widow and the orphan while uprooting the wicked's way." For these divine goals to be realized, Eights and others must join in the task.

While Judaism forbids taking the law into our own hands, it commands us to intervene when someone's life or safety is being directly threatened. Deuteronomy teaches us not to stand idly by the blood of our brothers and sisters. Therefore, we are charged with raising our voice against oppression and political persecution wherever and to whomever they occur. Many organized groups within the Jewish community dedicate themselves to this task, whether or not the endangered people are Jewish.

Judaism always sanctions legitimate self-defense. However, the example of the Exodus reminds us that God sides with the oppressed, not the oppressors. *Olam Ha'asiyah/*Conformist Eights (and all Jews) should be especially sensitive to the alienated, for we were "strangers in the land of Egypt."

TIKKUN/REPAIR

Given that Eights are prone to excess, sexual license and vulgarity, Cordevero offers the following in *Tomer Devorah:*

Now how shall one train himself in the quality of *Yesod?* Man should be careful in his speech so as not to bring him to thoughts that could lead to [licentious] emissions. It is needless to add that one should refrain from coarse speech; one must guard against even clean language which may titillate.

Eights' Security Point is Two, the caregiver. To become more caring and less hostile, Eights should be tender and sexually faithful, sanctifying the exclusivity of his marital relationship.

The quality of *Yesod* is the sign of the covenant [alluding to the Covenant of Abraham, Brit, whose sign is the circumcised male organ] ... Emissions must be saved for procreation ... man should not cause himself to become erect except with his wife, in cleanliness when the moment is proper for true coupling.

By giving themselves in sanctity and trust to their mates, Eights can let show those feelings of vulnerability and weakness which they have avoided. In such a supportive relationship, they can begin to claim their lost virtue of *Innocence*.

Desiring to truly protect rather than control those for whom they care, Eights, more than others, can take the primal force, *Yesod,* and use it to ascend toward the higher *Olam Ha Beriah*/Interindividual stage as champions of righteousness. By so doing, they coalesce the divine radiance, the *Shefa,* from all the *sefirot* above and channel it effectively through *Malchut* to mediate blessings to our world below.

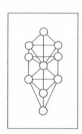

14

Point Nine: Shechinah— Divine Presence

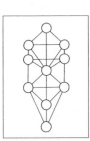

NINES HAVE BEEN LABELED **PEACE-makers, Mediators** or **Accommodators.** Haunted by a world that makes them feel ignored or unimportant, Nines have lost their essential connection to an unconditional **Love** which would provide equality and oneness of all. Their fixation of **Indolence** and passion of **Sloth** develop as they lazily seem to forget their own priorities and seek unity by merging with the needs of others. Instinctually, Nines can become absorbed on all levels with a mate and achieve **Union** in an intimate relationship. For a sense of fellowship, Nines seek **Participation** in social groups and show an **Appetite** for secondary interests and insubstantial diversions to replace real wants and needs in the area of personal well-being.

The *sefirah* that corresponds to Point Nine is *Shechinah,* divine presence or repose. Like Love, its corresponding

Holy Idea, *Shechinah* represents the warm, receptive Presence of Being, personified in Kabbalistic literature as a lovely, lovable sister or bride. Points Two and Nine both tend to merge with others, being more aware of others' wants than of their own desires. Kabbalists similarly compare *Binah* and *Shechinah,* describing both as the feminine aspects of the *sefirotic* system. As previously noted, *Binah* is the active female principle that, like the Two, has a controlling aspect and selectively alters its presentation to each of the successive *sefirot* that emerge from it. Like Nines, *Shechinah* is the harmonizing principle, which synthesizes the divine energy channeled to it from the *sefirot* above. Also a mediator, *Shechinah* is the conduit through which divine balance and a Sabbathlike peace descend on the world below.

PERSONALITY AND ITS TRAITS

Because they are easygoing and accepting, Nines are generally liked by all. Their nonthreatening gentleness and patience gives others a sense of peace and tranquility. Because they are receptive to all points of view, they lack arrogance, can offer direct, simple insights and can be particularly effective in resolving conflict.

Occupying the center position in the Eight-Nine-One *Belly Centered* triad (See Chapter Three for further details on the Triads), Nines are caught between being "bad children" and "good children," between alienating others and submitting to them. This paralysis is increased because they are also the pivot point between the approval-seeking Three and the anti-authoritarian Six in the Enneagram's self-enclosed core triangle. These conflicting tensions, therefore, make personal choice very difficult for Nines. It becomes easier to stall than to anger others and say "No," to seem to go along rather than to submit while trying to reach one's own decision.

Feeling that they were overlooked as children and not having attracted attention even when they got angry,

Nines, in effect, "spaced out." Caught between different factions and unable to effect change, Nines can see the validity of all positions, yet they wonder if it is valid for *them* to take a position at all. Therefore, Nines find it easier to worry about making a decision than to make one. They adopt a variety of strategies that make them appear to have low energy and be slow moving. They can sidetrack themselves by filling their schedules with things of secondary importance, thus delaying important decisions. They can establish rituals and habits with which they conduct their lives, exhibiting just enough energy to go through the motions without truly investing themselves in whatever they are doing. They can occupy their time with energy-draining activities such as watching television, drinking or substance abuse. Even the accumulation of responsibilities can be used to divert Nines from their own real priorities.

In relationships, Nines look to others to help them determine their wants. They seek to know their partners in-depth, and then adopt their partners' values and outlooks as their own. Merging with the other until their own point of view is obscured, Nines might continue relationships out of habit because ending the relationship could make Nines feel as if parts of themselves have been lost. Exerting power through passive aggression, Nines can stubbornly keep others from forcing them into making decisions and then be just as stubborn about holding onto those decisions once they are made. Nines have described their nature in the following way:

> "Being with someone is like being absorbed into their being."
>
> "I forget the source of my own interest and get dragged along on other people's trips."
>
> "Saying what I want if it differs from others makes me feel like I want to die."
>
> "Anger comes as a feeling of stubbornness in the

face of demand when someone expects something. Don't expect, please ask."

Qualities of the Nine at the *Tsadik* level emerge as modesty, stability, serenity, and an openness that lets them mediate healing and peace in conflict situations. Moderately developed *Benoni* Nine characteristics manifest as self-effacement, passivity, accommodation, and a denial of real threats in the hope that problems will disappear if everyone would just agree. *Rashah* Nine traits appear as self-degradation, helplessness, fatalism, resistance to help, and even disengagement from reality.

ASCENDING THROUGH THE *OLAMOT*
At the Conformist/*Olam Ha'asiyah* level, Nines seem asleep to their own inner needs, sure that they are not really important and that their efforts will not be valued. Psychologically and spiritually, they merge their identities with the groups and individuals with whom they are involved, letting others shape their preferences and opinions. Devoid of strong personal positions, they usually see validity in all sides of an issue and remain neutral in the midst of conflict. To maintain their comfort zone, they lower their energy and accommodate others' agendas. Even when they are very busy, chances are their activities reflect the priorities of others rather than their own conscious choice. To elude confrontation, they deny their own negative feelings, particularly anger. Rather than face those feelings, openly disagree, and potentially risk a fight they avoid or delay making decisions. They allow their attention to wander and fill their time with trivial diversions or assent, and then act *sub rosa* in a passive-aggressive, contrary manner.

Approaching the Conscientious/*Olam Ha Yetsirah* stage, Nines begin to recognize their fear of being overwhelmed by others' agendas and their anger at having suppressed their needs. Differentiating themselves, they start to distinguish among their feelings and recognize the difference between automatic habit and conscious choice. If other types are expanding their perspectives and breaking habitual patterns at this stage, Nines are now recognizing their own patterns of thought and prioritizing their ideas amid their all-inclusive purview. Growing clearer about their goals, they eschew former diversions and begin to see themselves as efficient, productive people. Valuing themselves as lovable, they become freer to choose the nature and extent of their relationships rather than merging into the desires and agendas of others. While better knowing what they want can be liberating, Nines at this stage may also feel isolated and afraid now that they are no longer merely handing over their lives.

Amid inner conflict and seemingly irreconcilable outer forces, Interindividual/*Olam Ha Beriah* Nines are able to take clear personal stands while being warmly receptive to others and their views. Having an expanded, strengthened view of themselves, they feel profoundly free to embrace or terminate relationships, rather than go through the motions merely to avoid conflict. Able to discern differences without creating confrontation, they make effective mediators who consciously use their ability to merge as a means to understand and care for others. Driven by empathy and compassion, they are able to concentrate their attention and mobilize their energies as they contribute to making this a better, more harmonious world.

THE BIBLICAL HEROINE: RACHEL

Among a variety of possible incarnations (King David being the most outstanding), Kabbalists have identified *Shechinah*, the *sefirah* that corresponds to Point Nine, with the matriarch Rachel. The translation of her name, "Little Lamb," suggests the degree of passivity found in *Olam Ha'asiyah*/Conformist Nines.

In the Bible, Rachel always appears in the context of relationship to another: As Laban's daughter and shepherdess; as Jacob's beloved and wife; as Leah's younger sister and rival; as Joseph's mother. She even dies while giving life to another, her younger son, Benjamin. Far more receptive than aggressive, Rachel is usually acted upon. Although she has brothers and an older sister, she is the one who is sent off to tend sheep. She is kissed and embraced by her cousin Jacob, whom she had never met, and quickly becomes the object of his yearning and labors. On her wedding day, her father manipulates her so that Leah can take her place as the bride.

As a Nine, Rachel could be simple and very direct once she had reached a decision. Tormented by her infertility, she demands of Jacob, "Give me children or I shall die." Wanting her sister's aphrodisiac mandrakes, she gains them by trading Jacob's attentions for that night to Leah. In true passive/aggressive fashion, Rachel sits upon her father's idols and stubbornly refuses to budge so that Laban won't find them during his search for them.

If *Binah* is Supernal mother, *Shechinah* is envisioned by the Kabbalists as a bride or sister. She is identified with *K'lal Yisrael* encompassing the disparate spirits of the corporate reality of the Jewish people. When Kabbalists liken the twenty-two pathways of the *Etz Chayim* (see Diagram 1) to a system of rivers, *Shechinah* serves as the sea or pool into which the *sefirotic* tributaries flow. In *Olam Ha Beriah/* Interindividual Nine fashion, she purposely blends their waters and, in turn, mediates their blessing to the world below.

Seen by the prophet Jeremiah as standing at Ramah and tearfully awaiting her exiled children, Rachel is the healing, unifying matriarch of Israel.

*SHA'AR/*GATEWAY

There is an adage that states when a Jew says "*I,*" he really says "*we.*" Almost every single petitionary prayer and confessional in Judaism is phrased in the first person plural. When Jews celebrate, they thank God, who has "kept *us* in life ..." When they beat their chests and recite the list of sins on Yom Kippur each says, "For the sin *we* have committed before You ..."

For Nines and others who treasure group participation, Judaism is a highly communal religion. Not only is this reflected in the phrasing of our liturgy, it speaks to the essence of our prayer quorums (*minyan*). Only when ten or more adult Jews pray together does God's special presence dwell among them. Together, they embody *K'lal Yisrael,* the corporate reality of the whole Jewish people. By joining together, they establish the proper ritual setting where the Torah can be read and where special prayers of sanctifying God, including the Mourner's Kaddish, can be recited. Leviticus teaches that God is sanctified in the midst of the people Israel.

While participating in the community is a prime Jewish value, Judaism reminds *Olam Ha'asiyah*/Conformist Nines and the rest of us of our unique intrinsic value. Each of us is needed to make up the communal whole and no one else can take our place. Perhaps this is why God created but a single human "in the beginning."

TIKKUN/REPAIR

Of all the instruction given by Cordevero to the various *sefirot* types, his spiritual tasks for Nines initially seem most puzzling. Given the self-denying personality traits of Nines, common wisdom counsels that they pay attention to themselves and their own needs. Yet in *Tomer Devorah,* Cordevero states:

> First and foremost ... take no pride in possessions ...
> think of [yourself] as abandoned ... [your] heart should
> be submissive and [your] habits abstemious.

On the surface, this spiritual advice would seem to feed the Nine's personality fixation rather than to prompt growth. However, a closer examination of Cordevero's writing indicates that he is not counseling that we abase ourselves before the needs of others, but instead, he advises humility, especially in prayer and before God. As such, Nines are not less worthy of attention than others, since everyone should stand in awe of the Creator of all who observes each of our deeds.

Cordevero prescribes a novel approach for Nines to move toward the higher *Olamot*/Stages by confronting their avoidance of change and confrontation. Drawing on the imagery of the *Shechinah* exiled from the rest of the *Etz Chayim* after the Fall, Nines should emulate the *Shechinah* and voluntarily leave home on a spiritual quest:

> One should go into voluntary banishment, from place
> to place, for the sake of the Name of Heaven; and thus
> he will become a chariot to the exiled *Shechinah*, Just
> as Rabbi Simeon and his associates used to do in
> order to engage in the study of Torah.

Cordevero observes that the more exertion one puts into this quest, the greater the benefit. Such effort should lead to fear and reverence of the Almighty, a fear that differs from normal concern for suffering, disaster or punishment. This awe of God should come from recognizing God's greatness, from acting as if all our actions are observed and from worry lest our misdeeds foul the heavens above and debase God's immanent presence, the *Shechinah*.

Cordevero draws on the metaphor of *Shechinah* as an exiled bride who needs to be restored to the blessing of union with the rest of the *Etz Chayim*. By engaging in the Virtuous *Right Action* of Loving-kindness, Justice, and Mercy, Nines can effect balance between the Right and Left Pathways of the *Etz Chayim*. Aided by prayer, Torah study and wearing *tefillin* (phylacteries worn daily on head and arm containing four scriptural passages) and *tallit* (a prayer shawl), the proper measure of divine radiance from each pathway can be conveyed to the *Shechinah*. Such a quest for sanctity can, in turn, infuse one's own marital relation with divine emulation and summon the *Shechinah* to be your divine companion when temporarily separated from your spouse.

Returning
to God

15

Keter: *Divine Crown,*
Our Transition to the Divine

Olam Ha'atsilut: The Integrated World

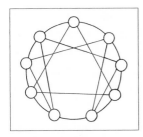 AN INSIGHT COMMON TO THE Kabbalah and the Enneagram is that each of us potentially embodies all the qualities of each personality type in the *sefirot* or the Enneagram. Although each of us is blessed with our own dominant style or particular *sefirah,* which is the root of our soul, we can manifest, in some way, all of these potentialities. Those unique individuals who ascend toward *Olam Ha'asiyah,* the fourth world/ stage, so integrate these qualities that their lives appear as seamless unities of action, mutuality, and intimacy. Their concerns are universal in scope, embracing the broad needs of humanity and our world.

As described in the preceding chapters, the journey through the first three *Olamot*/Stages, from the Conformist through the Conscientious to the Interindividual, represents a refining, breaking open, and reconstituting of the personality. Using terminology originated by the sixteenth-century Christian mystic John of the Cross, and now commonly employed in Western spirituality, the transition from the Conformist to the Conscientious stage embodies a "Dark Night of the Senses." As we have seen, this is a time of confusion, when repressed emotions begin to erupt and the way our acquired personalities previously helped us navigate our worlds no longer proves tenable. Another unsettling dynamic can accompany the move through the Conscientious into the Interindividual stage. Called "the Dark Night of the Soul," it is a period of profound uncertainty when, as shown above, even our spiritual practice and ways of serving God may change. We may feel unable to go back to our formerly preferred modes of divine service. Furthermore, our ways of experiencing God may also change, becoming both deeper and more inclusive. For example, Sixes who may have envisioned God as an authoritative Parent assuring certainty, may come to know God as a caring Companion who engenders the development of their own trust in the midst of uncertainty. Similarly, Twos who may have understood God to be the Rescuer of others in trouble might now experience God more intimately as the One Who both tenderly holds them and Who challenges them to act not only helpfully but justly.[4]

The ascent toward the fourth world/stage marks a decentering of the personality, a lived response to the realization that none of us is the hub of the universe, that our lives are ultimately not about ourselves. Given that only the Messiah's soul comes from *Keter Elyon,* the highest *sefirah* of the highest world, it is likely that no mortal can ever fully attain *Olam Ha'atsilut,* the Integrated stage. Only a rare few have even come close. However, Cordevero does offer a number of spiritual exercises for those willing to radically expand their understanding of God, deconstruct their personalities, and take the first steps, no matter how faltering, toward the fourth world.

In the first chapter of *Tomer Devorah,* we find a selection from scripture that Kabbalists have understood as a statement of the Supernal Attributes of the Compassionate Divine:

> Who is God like You, pardoning iniquity and forgiving transgression to the remnant of God's heritage. God does not maintain anger forever, but delights in lovingkindness. God will again show us compassion, vanquish our iniquities and cast all sin into the sea. Show faithfulness to Jacob, lovingkindness to Abraham as You have pledged to our ancestors from days of old.
>
> *Micah 7:18–20*

Cordevero breaks this passage into thirteen sections and, although written in ethnocentric language, interprets each as a quality of a God Who is at once universally just, ultimately merciful, and radically forgiving. He also teaches that these attributes must impel us to emulate the divine.

> It behooves man to aspire to be like unto his Creator, to enter into the mystery of the Supernal Form [*Adam Kadmon*], both in Image and Likeness.... For the importance of the Supernal Image and Likeness is in its deeds.

To actualize the Supernal Form in which we are fashioned, we must strive for equity, show forbearance toward those who harm us, and recognize the Divine that inheres in all persons and situations. Cordevero's most stirring images of this universal interconnection reveal the familial kinship between humans and God and depict the soul of each person at a prayer quorum as encompassing all other praying souls present at that time.

The second chapter of *Tomer Devorah* provides both negative and positive approaches to the move from the centrality of self toward the spiritual consciousness of *Olam Ha'atsilut*, the fourth world. His negative approach requires fleeing from honor and self gratification, a relentless confrontation of one's fixations and shortcomings, and the undertaking of penitential measures—short of compromising one's divine worship and scriptural study—which address those flaws, even if they prove painful and embarrassing. His positive approach is to respect every creature, to look for evidence of the Divine in every being and situation, and to open one's heart in universal love, even toward the wicked.

In the concluding section of *Tomer Devorah*, Cordevero indicates that different *sefirot* can be accessed at different times during the day. He prescribes a variety of spiritual tasks to be performed at certain hours so that each of us can help bring out the higher qualities of the appropriate *sefirah* at its prescribed time and integrate them as a seamless whole into our lives.

Night and its tranquil calm is the domain of *Malchut* or *Shechinah*, which is identified with Point Nine. This period has traditionally been equated with death, as if our souls have departed while we sleep. Drawing on scriptural command as well as on rabbinic and mystical practice, Cordevero counsels us to protect ourselves when retiring for the night by accepting the Yoke of God's Kingdom (*Malchut*) by reciting "*Shema Yisrael ...*" "Hear O Israel, the Lord our God, the Lord is One." We should then awake at midnight, ritually wash our hands, then seek to merge with *Shechinah* through studying Torah. This practice is know as *Tikkun Chatsot* (the Cosmic Repair at Midnight).

At dawn, we should worship in synagogue. Upon reaching the door of the synagogue, recite the verse from Psalms (5:8), "But as for me, in the abundance of Your Loving Kindness I come into Your House; I bow toward Your

Holy Palace in awe of You." This alludes to the three Patriarchs: Abraham, who embodies Loving-kindness (*Chesed* or *Gedulah,* Point Three); Isaac, who bows before Judgment (*Din* or *Gevurah,* Point Five); and Jacob, who recognized the awesome beauty of his Angelic Ladder dream at Beth El (*Tiferet,* Point Four). When standing in the synagogue, our intention (*Kavannah*) is to heal any conflict in the congregation, which itself incarnates *Shechinah,* God's indwelling Presence. Just as *Yesod,* Point Eight, acts as a channel that focuses and emits the divine radiance of *Shefa,* so should the worshipper act as a fountain of prayer, emitting praise of God from his mouth.

Since Abraham is credited with originating the morning service, it lets the worshipper identify with Abraham's Threelike quality of *Gedulah* or *Chesed.* During the day, Torah study, which includes Scripture (Point Six, *Netsach*) and the Rabbinic Code, *Mishnah* (Point Seven, *Hod*), helps us embody *Tiferet,* the Fourlike Beauty of Jacob. As dusk comes, we recite the *Minchah* afternoon service and identify with its reflective author Isaac, who mirrors *Din,* Point Five.

Even eating can be used to sanctify one's vitalistic, animal nature. If we observe the dietary laws (*Kashrut*) and also recite the appropriate table blessings, then the nourishment gained from foods can help lift us and our world toward God.

These daily practices help us identify with these *sefirot* and the Prevailing Light, Wisdom (*Chochmah,* Point One) and Understanding (*Binah,* Point Two), which will guide us throughout the day.[7]

The Face of God

Given the dynamics of our worldly existence, Cordevero, acknowledging that we need the qualities and skills of our personality types, states that "Man must perfect himself [in] ... those qualities [that] flow from the lower Powers.... "

Keter, the highest *sefirah*, integrates and transcends all those qualities. As the point of transition from the Essential, Limitless God, *Ayn Sof*, to the *sefirotic* qualities of the divine personality, it is also the point of convergence along the paths back from our fractured reality to a state of essential union. Those rare individuals who have ascended near the fourth world of *Atsilut* seem to embody the integrative qualities of *Keter* in their daily lives. For the rest of us, there are occasions when the spirit is freed from tension and distraction, when we too might temporarily reascend to both taste and evince the wholeness of *Keter*. Such times include moments of worship and contemplation, Shabbat time, and Holy Days.

Cordevero pictures those who so ascend as embodying the Face of God, a face whose traits we can correlate to the Enneagram Virtues. Since *Keter* is envisioned as the crown of *Adam Kadmon's* head, Cordevero relates these Virtues to the head's crown and the features below. First and foremost, the crown is bowed in *Humility*, which manifests patience, the utmost degree of mercy and the *Courage* to do good for others regardless of any obstacle. *Non-attachment* to honor, prestige, material goods or the false superiority of self-worth helps produce humility. *Sobriety* dismisses the options of vain, ugly or judgmental thoughts and dwells upon God's greatness, goodness and how we can steadily do good.

Rather than "harden" one's face against other people and doing irreparable harm through anger, *Innocence* comes through mild action and quelling anger in ourselves and others. *Honesty* refuses to entertain the false and the unworthy, by hearing (and doing) only the good, the helpful, the true. Forgiving transgressions and being patient even with unworthy people reflects *Serenity*, which breathes life, not anger. One's countenance radiates *Equanimity* by receiving with calm pleasantness anything which comes our way. Finally, *Right Action* flows from speaking well and not being diverted by idle or unkind words.

The simultaneous embodiment of all these virtues is subsumed by Cordevero under what he considers to be the major virtue, *Humility*. The inspiration and result of this state is the respectful recognition that the wisdom of God's creation is in each of God's creatures and that "it behooves man to plant the love of Humankind in his heart."

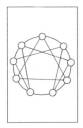

16

A Meditation on the Return to Ayn Sof

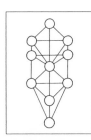 CAN WE, EVERYDAY MEN AND WOMEN, embody the Divine in our lives? Each of us derives the root of our soul from a specific *sefirah,* yet we each personify all the potential of *Adam Kadmon.* How might we identify the passions that obscure these higher traits within us so that we might transcend them and experience, if fleetingly, a sense of union with the Divine?

Psalm 62 states, "Indeed, for God let my soul be still." Perhaps it is through quieting our minds and spirits that we reveal the divine within us and beyond us. The following meditation might prove a helpful starting point on your road back to Essence:

Diagram 2 depicts the location of the *sefirot* along *Adam Kadmon.*

DIAGRAM 2

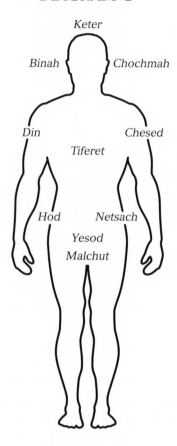

Since we have correlated the Enneagram Personality Type Points to the *sefirot,* we can now locate the points along the body from a Kabbalistic standpoint.

Point One	Perfectionists' *Chochmah*	Right Eye
Point Two	Caregivers' *Binah*	Left Ear
Point Three	Achievers' *Gedulah (Chesed)*	Right Arm
Point Four	Romantics' *Tiferet*	Heart
Point Five	Observers' *Din (Gevurah)*	Left Arm
Point Six	Loyalists' *Netsach*	Right Leg

Point Seven	Adventurers' *Hod*	Left Leg
Point Eight	Confrontationists' *Yesod*	Genitals
Point Nine	Mediators' *Shechinah*	Genitals

During our meditation, we will pause at each of these locations as we envision the *Shefa,* the radiant energy of *Ayn Sof* descending through our bodies. At each spot, we will examine how the passion associated with the corresponding Point manifests itself in our lives.

For example, when we reach our right leg, which is identified with Point Six, or *Netsach,* we will explore the Six's passion, Fear. We will ask ourselves three times, "How are you fearful?" and wait silently for responses from within. It is interesting to note how different personality types refract the passions of others through the lens of their own concerns. In questions about fear, Sixes might respond that they are afraid of physical danger or the harmful intentions of others. Threes, however, might indicate that they, as Achievers, fear failure, while the confrontationist Eights might fear appearing vulnerable and weak. These responses correspond to the Kabbalistic idea that each *sefirah* contains within it the traits of all other *sefirot* moderated by special characteristics of that given *sefirah.*

Just as we will trace the descent of the *Shefa* through our bodies, so we will trace its reascent back to *Ayn Sof.* At each *sefirah* location, we will offer a "healing verse" from Jewish liturgy or scripture which will express the higher qualities of that particular Point. The meditation will conclude by leading us into a sense of union with *Ayn Sof.*

The meditation is divided into seven sections, beginning with Sunday and culminating on Saturday, the Shabbat. Here are some practical suggestions about how to proceed:

- Allow yourself at least thirty minutes of uninterrupted silence for the meditation each day.

Choose a time when you can be relaxed, but alert.

- Find a comfortable place where you will not be disturbed.

- Choose a position, be it seated, kneeling, lotus or prone in which your head, heart and belly, the seats of our Three Centers of Intelligence or levels of soul, can be aligned comfortably and straight.

- Close your eyes or gaze ahead in a soft, unfocused manner.

- Begin with some gentle breathing, exhaling through your mouth twice the volume of air you inhale through your nose.

- If you can, memorize the passions or the healing verses for that day. If not, you might record the guidance for that day on a tape recorder and play it back to help lead your meditation. Speak slowly and allow for several seconds of silence on the tape where pauses are indicated by a series of three periods.

- Keep a journal in which you can reflect on the questions at the end of each day's meditation. Review your journal each day before beginning the next meditation. While no journal questions will be given for Shabbat, the day of rest, you might wish to reflect on that day about your meditative experiences that occurred during the entire preceding week.

Now let us begin.

Sunday
Yom Rishon—The First Day

Imagine *Ayn Sof,* the boundless, seamless Divine, hovering over your head as a bright, luminous cloud....

If you can, visualize its color ... its texture ... its radiance ...

Slowly, a beam of light shines forth from the cloud, a beam of *Shefa,* the radiant energy of God.... Trace the beam as it enters your body through the crown of your head....

Feel the light illuminate your right eye, which can see the beauty of all things, but too often sees only flaws and imperfections.... Ask your eye:

"How are you angry?" Then probe deeper:

"Of what are you angry?"

"Why are you angry?"

Having listened to your inner voice, feel the light brighten your face as it moves to your left ear, which can hear even the unspoken needs of others. More often, though, it listens to flattery and for ways to manipulate others. Ask your ear:

"How are you prideful?"

"Of what are you prideful?"

"Why are you prideful?"

Relax in the silence of your answers and when you are ready, return to yourself.

Journal Questions

- What color and texture did you sense in the cloud?

- Did you experience any sensations when the light entered your body? When it illumined your eye? Your ear? Did you sense any resistance to the light?

• What answers came to mind concerning your anger? Your pride?

Monday
Yom Sheni—The Second Day

Envision the cloud of *Ayn Sof* above you ... see its light move through your forehead ... your eye ... your ear....

Now feel the light of *Shefa* move from your left ear down your neck.... Now it moves across your shoulder and illuminates your right arm....

Your right arm can accomplish great things, yet can push others aside as it pursues its goals. Ask your arm:

"How are you deceitful?"

"With what are you deceitful?"

"Why are you deceitful?"

Having heard your answers, sense the radiance from the *Ayn Sof* transverse your shoulder and fill your heart, which knows the depths of emotion, but can be shattered by longing and jealousy. Ask your heart:

"How are you envious?"

"Of what are you envious?"

"Why are you envious?"

Now feel the light move to brighten your left arm, which can categorize and set things in proper order, yet too often hoards your resources and fends off others. Ask your arm:

"How are you stingy?"

"With what are you stingy?"

"Why are you stingy?"

Relax in the silence of your answers and when you are ready, return to yourself.

Journal Questions

- What answers did you receive to the questions concerning your deceit? Your envy? Your stinginess?

- What did you experience in your arms and heart when they were filled with the light? After the light moved on?

Tuesday
Yom Shlishi—The Third Day

Envision the cloud of *Ayn Sof* above you. See the divine light from the cloud move through your head to your eye ... your ear ... your arms ... your heart....

Now feel the *Shefa* move slowly down your spine....

See it illumine your right leg, which can stand firm and true, but instead often runs scared from perceived threats or runs directly into danger to prove that it is not afraid. Ask your leg:

"How are you fearful?"

"Of what are you fearful?"

"Why are you fearful?"

Sense the light move across your hips to your left leg, which can joyously explore all the adventures and experiences of life, but often flees from commitment. Ask your left leg:

"How are you gluttonous?"

"For what are you gluttonous?"

"Why are you gluttonous?"

Now feel the light move to the place in your lower body, where you locate the masculine within you. That locale can be strong and forthright or domineering and excessive. Ask it:

"How are you lustful?"

"Of what are you lustful?"

"Why are you lustful?"

Finally, the light moves to that place where you sense the feminine within you. That locale can detect the good in various opinions from others, but too often is unaware of your own real needs. Ask it:

"How are you unaware?"

"Of what are you unaware?"

"Why are you unaware?"

Journal Questions

- What answers did you receive to the questions about fear? Gluttony? Lust? Being unaware of yourself?

- Where did you locate in your body the generative power of the opposite gender? What did you experience when you questioned that locale?

Wednesday
Yom Revii—The Fourth Day

On Wednesday, time accelerates as we move closer to Shabbat. On this day, the fourth day of Creation, the sun, moon and stars were formed. The very celestial bodies whose movement lets us measure the passage of time. Today, we begin the reascent of the *Shefa* through our bodies back to *Ayn Sof*.

Sense the divine light streaming from *Ayn Sof* above through the crown of your head.... Feel it stream from your eye ... your ear ... your arms ... your heart ... down through your spine ... to your legs....

Envision, if you can, these beams of light merging

together in your lower abdominal region. Here, the lights blend ... and rest ... and harmonize and grow stronger.

Address this place of peace, of harmony, of repose, this place where you locate the feminine in your lower body:

"From repose ascend toward the heavens and sanctify God's name."

Feel the *Shefa* move to the place where you locate the masculine within you. Tell this place of male generative power and strength:

"Act righteously and you support the world."

The radiance now travels to your left leg, that leg which seeks adventure, yet tries to flee responsibility. Tell this leg:

"Keep faith with God's commands and you can explore all God's paths."

Finally, the light rests on your right leg, the leg that can offer loyal support or run in fear. Tell this leg:

"Stand firm and you shall see the salvation of the Lord."

As your lower body is illuminated by the divine radiance, rest in the light. When you are ready, return to yourself.

Journal Questions

- Did you notice any change in feeling as the light began to ascend? What did you experience?

- Did any of your limbs resist the reascent of the light or the "healing verse?" If so, what do you think caused that resistance?

Thursday
Yom Chamishi—The Fifth Day

Feel your lower body glow with the radiance of the divine....

Slowly the *Shefa* moves up your spine and across your left shoulder. It fills your left arm, the arm that can be stingy and keep others at bay. Tell that arm:

"Open your hand and satisfy, willingly, all of life."

The radiance now travels from your arm to fill your heart, which can be divided by longing and envy. Tell your heart:

"Unite our heart that we might love and revere."

Now the brilliance moves to your right arm, the arm that can create illusions or accomplish great things. Tell your arm:

"With your right arm exalt God. Your right arm can perform valiant deeds."

As the divine light illuminates your chest and your arms, relax in the silence. When you are ready, return to yourself.

Journal Questions

- Was the sense of light in your torso and arms today different from the light in your lower body yesterday? If so, how?

- How did your arms and heart respond when addressed?

Friday
Yom Shishi—The Sixth Day

As you anticipate the arrival of Shabbat, sense the light from the *Ayn Sof* in your legs and lower body. Feel it as it moves up your spine ... filling your left arm ... your heart ... your right arm....

The radiance now illuminates your neck and travels to your left ear, which can hear others' unspoken needs, but listens too often to flattery. Tell your ear:

"Hear our voices and act with mercy and compassion toward us."

As the light glows from your face, feel it brighten your right eye, which sees all the possibilities and flaws of the world. Tell that eye:

"Enlighten our eyes, God, with Your divine guidance."

As your head shines with the radiance of the Lord, rest in the silence. When you are ready, return to yourself.

Journal Questions

- What sensations did you experience as the light moved to your head?

- What response did your ears offer to the verse you told it? Your eye?

Saturday
Yom Shabbat—The Holy Shabbat

Envision the radiant, luminous cloud of *Ayn Sof*, the boundless, seamless God, hovering over you on this Shabbat.

The light enters you through your forehead and slowly, the brilliance of God illuminates your right eye.

Sense the light's path as it travels to your left ear ... down your neck ... filling your right arm ... your heart ... your left arm....

Mark the light's journey as it moves down your spine ... shining forth from your right leg ... your left leg....

See the paths of light streaming from each limb and organ all merging together in your lower body....

Now the light begins its ascent. It moves ever more quickly from your hips and legs up your spine ... to your heart ... your arms ... your neck and your ear ... and your eye....

As the light ascends through your forehead in a single, brilliant beam, you feel your entire self ascend with it as you merge into the boundless, seamless light of Essence, the unity of *Ayn Sof....*

Rest in the brilliance of God and in the Wholeness of Shabbat.

Shabbat Shalom.

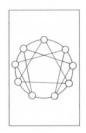

Epilogue
Tseh U'Lemad—
Go Forth and Learn

A rabbinic story tells of a seeker who came to Hillel, the famous first-century sage. He posed the same question that he had asked Hillel's more acerbic colleague, Shammai, who had sent him away in disgust. "Teach me the entire Torah while standing on one foot." Rather than rise to the bait, Hillel instead rose to the challenge. He stated, "Do not do to your fellow what is hateful to you. The rest is commentary. Go forth and learn."

Many students of Judaism quote only the first clause of Hillel's dictum. They note that he has recast the Golden Rule, "Do unto others as you would have them do to you," in the negative, enjoining us from harming others rather than presumptuously assuming that what we like they will too. They claim that Hillel has encapsulated the entire Torah in one phrase. Yet perhaps the most telling part of Hillel's statement is his parting charge: *Go forth and learn.*

If this brief overview of the Enneagram and Kabbalah has piqued your interest the challenge is now to take up the work. For those wishing to read more about the Enneagram, a comprehensive bibliography can be found in Jerome Wagner's *The Enneagram Spectrum of Personality Styles* (Portland, Ore: Metamorphous Press, 1996). The first text written on the Enneagram from a Jewish perspective is Miriam Adahan's *Awareness* (New York: Feldheim, 1994). Hannah Nathans's *The Enneagram at Work: Towards Personal Mastery and Social Intelligence* (Schiedam, The Netherlands: Scriptum, 2003) provides some interesting new ways to map the *Etz Chayim,* the four worlds, and their attendant Levels of Consciousness. To ascertain your Enneagram point, a number of questionnaires are available, including my own *Cast In God's Image: Discovering Your Personality Type Using the Enneagram and Kabbalah* (Woodstock, VT: Jewish Lights Publishing, 2001), David Daniels's and Virginia Price's *The Essential Enneagram: The Definitive Personality Test and Self-Discovery Guide* (New York: HarperCollins, 2000). P. J. & D. Aspell's *The Enneagram Inventory* (San Antonio: Lifewings, 2000) and Don Richard Riso's *Discovering Your Personality Type* (Boston: Houghton Mifflin, 2003). A more detailed exploration of your own Type and inner map may be gained by attending sessions and having a personal interview with a teacher trained in the Oral Tradition by Helen Palmer of Berkeley, California.

A host of books are available concerning Kabbalah which are very different from each other. One of my favorite introductions is David Ariel's *The Mystic Quest* (Northvale, NJ: Jason Aronson, 1990). The works of Gershom Scholem and Moshe Idel are among the best academic work available on Jewish mysticism. English language texts on Kabbalistic practices include Yitzhak Buxbaum's, *Jewish Spiritual Practices* (Northvale, NJ: Jason Aronson, 1994), David Cooper's *The Handbook of Jewish Meditation Practices* (Woodstock, VT: Jewish Lights Publishing, 2000), Aryeh Kaplan's, *Jewish Meditation* (New York: Schocken Books, 1995), and *Meditation from the Heart of Judaism: Today's Teachers Share Their Practices, Techniques, and Faith* (Woodstock, VT: Jewish Lights Publishing, 1999). Moshe Cordevero's *The Palm Tree of Deborah* (Southfield, MI: Targum, 1993) was beautifully translated and annotated by Moshe Miller.

One final note: In July 1995, I attended three lectures in Chicago by Hebrew University's Dr. Moshe Idel, the world's foremost scholar in the academic study of Kabbalah. When asked how people should begin their Jewish mystical quest, Idel answered simply, "learn Hebrew."

Far from being curt or dismissive, Idel's advice was challenging and profound. Some seekers today dismiss

Judaism as a spiritual path. Perhaps they remember He-brew School as boring. Or maybe the Judaism to which they were exposed was spiritually unsatisfying. Or maybe Judaism doesn't seem as appealing as paths that are more exotic and to which they are now devoting considerable adult energy, time and inquiry.

An examination of Cordevero's spiritual tasks reveals that they are the stuff of which normative Jewish life is composed: Torah study, worship, dedication to communal institutions, caring family relations and repentance. In ad-dition to prescribing different practices for different *se-firot,* Cordevero reconnected the practices to their pristine Covenantal purpose: purifying the human character and soul; communing with others and with God through Torah, worship and loving deeds; identifying with the Di-vine and strengthening the power of the Holy Presence in the heavens above and the world below.

None of us should wait until our knowledge of He-brew, scripture or the classical texts is complete to begin the practices in this book. Waiting will just postpone em-bracing the richness of a 4,000-year-old tradition which spawned and nourishes the Kabbalah. It will also post-pone enjoying the support and celebration that come with communal life. As Hillel told the seeker: Go forth and learn—and act as well.

Endnotes

Section I

1. D. R. Riso with R. Hudson, *Personality Types,* rev. ed. (Boston: Houghton Mifflin, 1996), 223.
2. This observation is based on two unusual uses of language in Genesis 2:7. The verb used there to describe God's fashioning of Adam is the same term used in Hebrew for character inclination (*Yetser*). Because the first letter of that term is doubled (*vaYYetser*), the sages of Israel claim that each human being has two character inclinations.
3. The phrase used in Exodus 34:29 to describe Moses's face is *karan* or *panav*. This literally translates as "skin of his face became hornlike." Since the word *karan* also means "ray of light," the text can connote that Moses's face toughened and/or beamed.
4. *Ma' amorot Avot* 5. The expression, "And God said, 'Let there be ...'" appears ten times in Genesis 1.
5. *Pesikta Rabbati,* vol. 608 a–b.
6. Babylonian Talmud *Hagigah* 12a: "R. Zutra b. Tibiah said that Rab said: By ten things (or words) was the world created: By wisdom and by understanding, and by reason, and by strength, and by rebuke, and by might, by righteousness and by judgment, by lovingkindness and by compassion." This list does differ from the later Kabbalistic formulation.
7. The full integration of the *sefirot* in *Olam Ha'atsilut* is reflected in the fact that in that world they are called *sefirot b'li-mah, sefirot* without individual actualization. The process by which they are individualized into interconnected but distinct *sefirot* in *Olam Ha Beriah* is known as *tzimtzum peruda,* the contraction of separation.

8. The best graphic I have seen depicting the overlay of the four worlds' Trees of Life is a poster entitled "Connectivity" based on a 1992 rendering by David Friedman, an Israeli artist.

9. Post-Zohar Kabbalists posited two additional levels of soul, *Chayyah* and *Yechidah,* representing our intuitive cognition and the aspect of our spirits which can merge with God. These are considered the psychological parallels of *Olam Ha'atsilut* and *Ayn Sof,* respectively.

10. James Webb, *The Harmonious Circle: The Lives and Work of G. I. Gurdjieff, P. D. Ouspensky, and Their Followers* (New York: G. P. Putnam's Sons, 1980), 510.

11. Ibid., 516–518.

12. K. V. Hurley and T. E. Dobson, *What's My Type?* (San Francisco: HarperCollins, 1991), 4, 5.

13. Riso with Hudson, *Personality Types,* 12, 13.

14. We are not suggesting that the road to Essence lies in recapturing a juvenile, childlike state. Rather it is the sense of unconflicted wholeness and spontaneity experienced during childhood that we seek to recover at the higher stages of personal growth through the authentic integration of our inner life and its harmonization with our actions in the outer world. For more on what has been termed the "Pre/Trans Fallacy," see Ken Wilber, *The Eye of Spirit: An Integral Vision for a World Gone Slightly Mad* (Boston: Shambala, 1997), chapters 6 and 7.

15. A fascinating panel discussion on how genetic predisposition can affect personality type and attention focusing from early infancy took place at the Enneagram Association Conference, Loyola University, Chicago, July 12–14, 1996. Of particular interest were studies cited by Russ Hudson and Dr. David Daniels. The idea that being born with an innate temperament limits how we apprehend the fullness of reality bolsters the insight found in some Kabbalistic and Christian texts that becoming physically incarnate in a body is the

Fall. Tapes of this session, "Childhood Development," are available from Credence Cassettes, 115 E. Armour Blvd., Kansas City, MO 64111.

16. Given that different persons and different types mentally filter their experiences differently, no one scenario can account for any one type. Extensive background possibilities for each type can be found in Jerome Wagner's *The Enneagram Spectrum of Personality Styles: An Introductory Guide* (Portland, OR: Metamorphous Press, 1996).

17. The self-descriptions of the various personality types in this text are paraphrases of two sources. Some are derived from my own Enneagram typing interviews conducted between October 1996 and July 1997. Others were taken from panel presentations conducted at the First International Enneagram Conference, Stanford University, August 1994. These presentations have been recorded as the "Nine Points of View" video series by the Workshops in the Oral Tradition with Helen Palmer, Berkeley, CA.

18. Riso with Hudson, *Personality Types*, 17–19. The entire Enneagram community is indebted to David Burke of Australia for highlighting the importance of Evagrius on the development of the Enneagram. For further information on the life and thought of Evagrius of Pontus, see www.scourmont.be.

19. Sandra Maitri, *The Spiritual Dimension of the Enneagram: Nine Faces of the Soul* (New York: Jeremy P. Tarcher/Putnam, 2000), 24–35.

20. The most thorough and accurate description of the Wings and their effect on each core personality type can be found in Riso with Hudson, *Personality Types*.

21. Helen Palmer, *The Enneagram: Understanding Yourself and the Others in Your Life* (San Francisco: HarperCollins, 1991), 49–51.

22. There has been a debate among practitioners of the Enneagram. Does movement against the arrow always

indicate personal growth and integration associated with the high traits of the Security Point? Does movement with the arrow indicate inevitable degeneration related to the baser traits of the Stress Point? Currently most practitioners also recognize that positive qualities can develop from the challenge of stress and negative aspects can arise because of past experiences or insecurity in dealing with a good opportunity. Additionally, there is an assertion that under extreme stress a person might "flip" into the lower qualities of his or her security point. According to this scenario, in extreme, is our One might become like a Seven who loses all sense of boundaries and commitment.

23. A. Z. Friedman, *Wellsprings of Torah* (New York: Judaica Press, 1990), 378.

24. Elizabeth Liebert, *Changing Life Patterns: Adult Development in Spiritual Direction* (Mahwah, NJ: Paulist Press, 1992), chapters 5–7.

25. Lawrence Kushner, *God Was in this Place and I, i Did Not Know: Finding Self, Spirituality and Ultimate Meaning* (Woodstock, VT: Jewish Lights, 1994), 173.

26. On *Merkhavat:* G. I. Gurdjieff, *Meetings with Remarkable Men* (New York: E. P. Dutton, 1969), 90. On Metatron: Helen Palmer, "The Vice to Virtue Conversion," Loyola University, Enneagram Association Conference (Credence Tapes, 1996).

27. For the influences of these schools on Kabbalah, see Moshe Idel, *Kabbalah: New Perspectives* (New Haven: Yale University Press, 1988), 9, 13, 15. G. G. Scholem, *Kabbalah* (New York: Times Books, 1974), 25, 27, 35, 37, 49.

28. Alternately, the name of the Holy Idea for Point Two is Freedom; for Point Four, Idealism; and for Point Seven, Work. For a complete description of the Holy Ideas and the reasons for their alternative names, see A. H. Almaas's *Facets of Unity: The Enneagram of Holy Ideas* (Berkely, CA: Diamond Work, 1998).

29. Related to me by Helen Palmer at her professional training seminar, August 1995, Menlo Park, CA. It is this reason that my ordering of the *sefirot* along the Enneagram is different from Kathleen Hurley and Theodore Dobson's earlier intuitive placement in *What's My Type?*, 151–152. My ordering also differs from that found in Richard Rohr's *Discovering the Enneagram: An Ancient Tool, a New Spiritual Journey* (New York: Crossroads, 1992), 229. Rohr correlates Point Five to *Yesod*, the base seminal *sefirah* and Point Eight to *Gevurah*, the power of Divine limitation and judgment. Although Five and Eight are joined by a line, I believe that Five better corresponds to the constricting, differentiating aspect of *Gevurah/Din* while Eight better parallels the male generative force of *Yesod*, which is also known as *Tsadik*, mirroring the Eight's emphasis on Justice.

Section II

1. The discussion of each type's traits is based on the Levels of Development that were discovered by Enneagram author Don Richard Riso in 1977. He and his co-author, Russ Hudson, have worked out nine distinct Levels for each type, grouped into healthy, average, and unhealthy ranges as I am discussing them here. For more information on the Levels of Development, see *Personality Types,* rev. ed., 1996.

2. While no written description can cover the unique spiritual journey of each type, James Empereur surely comes the closest in his magnificent text, *The Enneagram and Spiritual Direction: Nine Paths to Spiritual Direction* (New York: Continuum, 1997). While the correlations to Kabbalah are mine, the snapshot descriptions of each type at the various *Olamot*/Stages are largely drawn from his insightful writing.

3. Background information on Cordevero taken from J.

Ben-Shlomo's essay in G. G. Scholem's *Kabbalah,*
401–404. Translations of the *Tomer Devorah* used in
this text are adapted from Raphael Ben Zion's *The An-
thology of Jewish Mysticism* (New York, Judaica Press,
1981).

4. For a description of the changes in God concept for
each of the types, see Empereur's, *Enneagram and
Spiritual Direction.*

5. Louis Ginzberg, *Legends of the Jews,* vol. 1 (Philadel-
phia: Jewish Publication Society, 1937), 186–187.

6. Ibid.

7. For the correlation between the points, the biblical heroes, and the *sefirot,* see the preceding chapters. Although Cordevero does not explicitly mention the
sefirot of *Chochmah, Binah, Netsach,* and *Hod,* his use
of the terms "Prevailing Light" and "Study of Torah"
alludes to them.

Glossary of Terms

Enneagram

Acquired Personality—Our habitual pattern of thoughts, feelings and responses to life's situations, derived from our experience and our innate temperament. The acquired personality is necessary to negotiate through life, but can smother our real, essential self.

Arrows—The directional lines which connect the Enneagram Personality Type Points to each other. Movement with the arrow, such as 1—>4, is toward one's Stress Point. Movement against the arrow, such as 8<—2, is toward one's Security Point.

Enneagram—A nine-pointed star like diagram used to chart the unfolding of the human psyche.

Essence—The original, undivided unity of all being.

Essential Self—The aspect of self when we feel at one with the world, experiencing no conflicts between our thoughts, instincts, and emotions.

Fixation—The mental image we form to compensate for the particular aspect of Essence we feel we have lost.

Holy Idea—The aspect of Essence we feel we have lost while responding to the tensions and experiences of life.

Instinctual Subtype—A means of differentiating personalities within the same type based upon our three instincts for survival. Those most concerned with personal well-being are Self-Preservation Subtypes. Those most concerned with intimate relationships, the propagation of the species, are Sexual Subtypes. Those most concerned with issues of group status, one's place in the herd, are Social Subtypes.

Passion—Our chief emotional trait developed to compensate for the aspect of Essence we feel we have lost.

Point—The nine individual numbers on the Enneagram, each representing a different basic personality type. In Enneagram literature, these Points are also referred to as Type or Style.

Security Point—The personality type whose higher traits we emulate when we are feeling comfortable and secure. These are indicated by movement against the arrow within the Enneagram, so that 3<—6 indicates that Six is the Security Point of Three.

Stress Point—The personality type whose lower traits we exhibit when we experience distress. These are indicated by movement with the arrow, so that 2—>8 indicates that Eight is the Stress Point of Two.

Triads—The division of the nine Enneagram types into three groups of three based on their predominant personality faculties. Points Eight, Nine, and One are the Instinctual or "Belly Centered" triad, because persons of these types react to experience primarily through bodily instinct. Points Five, Six, and Seven are the "Head Centered" triad, because they respond primarily through thinking. Points Two, Three and, Four are the "Heart Centered" triad because they respond primarily through emotion.

Kabbalah

Adam Kadmon—The humanlike configuration of the ten traits of God's personality as Primordial Man, based on the idea that humans are shaped in the Divine image.

Arba Olamot—The "four worlds," or dimensions of reality, interposed between *Ayn Sof,* the infinite, unknowable Divine, and our world. The divine light of each successive descending world becomes ever more obscured as its coarseness and physicality increases. On the psychological level, the worlds have been correlated to the spiritual, intellectual, emotional, and instinctually active capacities of human beings.

Ayn Sof—The boundless, seamless, unknowable God.

Echad—The One God Who is the undivided, unlimited unity underlying all creation. *Echad* is sometimes used synonymously with *Ayn Sof.*

Etz Chayim—The configuration of the ten traits of God's personality as the Tree of Life.

Four Worlds—The theory that our physical world descended from God through four worlds of increasing physical coarseness. These four worlds are *Olam Ha'atsilut,* the World of Emanation; *Olam Ha Beriah,* the World of Creating; *Olam Ha Yetsirah,* the World of Formation; and *Olam Ha'asiyah,* the archetype of our World of Physical Action.

Netsotsot—Sparks of divine light which were scattered throughout the world during *shevirat ha kelim.* By performing God's commandments, *mitzvot,* with the proper intention, we can lift these sparks back to their source in the *Etz Chayim* and hasten world redemption.

Olam Ha'asiyah—One of the four worlds. *Olam Ha'asiyah* concerns the importance of attention to physicality, logistics, and grounding.

Olam Ha'atsilut—One of the four worlds. *Olam Ha'atsilut* is the transcendent dimension of the four aspects of spiritual practice found within Hasidic and Kabbalistic traditions. This is where you connect beyond the known or conceivable and experience pure, unified being.

Olam Ha Beriah—One of the four worlds; this one concerns ideas, thoughts, and innovations.

Olam Ha Yetsirah—One of the four worlds; this one deals with the formation and addressing of feelings.

Ratso Va-Shov—"Egress and Return." The continual movement of the divine radiance along the twenty-two pathways that connect the *sefirot* along the *Etz Chayim.*

Sefirot—The ten manifestations of the divine personality. For a detailed list and description of the *sefirot,* see Chapter Two.

Shefa—The divine radiant energy of *Ayn Sof* which flows along the twenty-two paths to the *sefirot.* The *sefirot,* in turn, mediate the blessings of the *Shefa* to our world below.

Shevirat ha kelim—"The Breaking of the Vessels." During Creation, the seven lower *sefirot* shattered because they could not contain the full radiant energy of the *Shefa*. This shattering caused the *Netsotsot* to scatter and helps account for the initial misalignment of the *Etz Chayim*.

Sitra Achra—"The Other Side." The reality of evil pictured as the shadow, mirror image of the *Etz Chayim*.

Three Levels of Soul—Derived from the three Hebrew words used for spirit. *Nefesh* represents our creature vitality and instinct; *Ruach* is our emotional and social self; and *Neshamah* embodies our speculative reason, reflective self-consciousness, and high intuition.

Tikkun—The performance of God's commandments with the intent to elevate the *Netsotsot* and help repair the cosmic fissures that occurred during *shevirat ha kelim*.

Tselem—Envisioned by Kabbalists as an ethereal body, it is likened to a garment of our characteristics and experiences which we weave through our deeds. Similar to the acquired personality, it contains both the light of our higher traits and the *Tsel*, the shadow side of our ignoble traits.

Yetser—"Inclination." According to rabbinic psychology, each individual has two inclinations. The *Yetser HaTov* is our Good Inclination, our altruistic drive. The *Yetser HaRa* is our Harmful Inclination, our drive toward self-aggrandizement at the expense of other people.

Suggested Readings

Enneagram

Adahan, Miriam. *Awareness*. New York: Feldheim, 1994.

Addison, Howard A. *Cast in God's Image: Discover Your Personality Type Using the Enneagram and Kabbalah*. Woodstock, Vt.: Jewish Lights Publishing, 2001.

Aspell, P.J., & D. Aspell. *The Enneagram Inventory*. San Antonio, Tex.: Life Wings, 2000.

Baron, R., & E. Wagele. *The Enneagram Made Easy*. San Francisco: HarperSanFrancisco, 1994.

Daniels, David. *The Stanford Enneagram Discovery Inventory & Guide*. Palo Alto, Calif.: Stanford University, 1997.

The Enneagram Monthly. For information call 877-428-9639.

Hurley, Kathy, & Ted Dobson. *What's My Type?* San Francisco: HarperSanFrancisco, 1992.

Lewis Lawida, D., & A. Lewis Lawida. *The Enneagram Workbook*. Scottsdale, Ariz.: Natron Publishing, 1995.

Liebert, Elizabeth. *Changing Life Patterns*. Mahwah: Paulist Press, 1992.

Palmer, Helen. *The Enneagram*. San Francisco: HarperSanFrancisco, 1991.

_____. *The Enneagram Advantage*. New York: Harmony, 1998.

_____. *The Enneagram in Love and Work*. San Francisco: HarperSanFrancisco, 1996.

_____. *The Pocket Enneagram*. San Francisco: HarperSanFrancisco, 1995.

Riso, Don Richard. *Discovering Your Personality Type*. Boston: Houghton Mifflin Co., 2003.

Riso, Don Richard, with Russ Hudson. *Personality Types*. Revised. Boston: Houghton Mifflin Co., 1996.

Rohr, Richard. *Enneagram II*. New York: Crossroads, 1998.

Rohr, Richard, with Andreas Ebert. *Discovering The Enneagram*. New York: Crossroads, 1992.

Wagner, Jerome. *The Enneagram Spectrum of Personality Styles*. Portland, Ore.: Metamorphous Press, 1996.

Kabbalah

Buxbaum, Yitzhak. *Jewish Spiritual Practices*. Northvale, N.J.: Jason Aronson, 1994.

Cooper, David. *The Handbook of Jewish Meditation Practices: A Guide for Enriching the Sabbath and Other Days of Your Life*. Woodstock, Vt.: Jewish Lights Publishing, 2000.

———. *God Is a Verb*. New York: Riverhead, 1998.

Davis, Avram, ed. *Meditation from the Heart of Judaism: Today's Teachers Share Their Practices, Techniques, and Faith*. Woodstock, Vt.: Jewish Lights Publishing, 1997.

Frankiel, Tamar. *The Gift of Kabbalah: Discovering the Secrets of Heaven, Renewing Your Life on Earth*. Woodstock, Vt.: Jewish Lights Publishing, 2003.

Green, Arthur. *Ehyeh: A Kabbalah for Tomorrow*. Woodstock, Vt.: Jewish Lights Publishing, 2004.

Idel, Moshe. *Kabbalah: New Perspectives*. New Haven, Conn.: Yale University, 1990.

Kaplan, Aryeh. *Jewish Meditation*. New York: Schocken, 1995.

Kushner, Lawrence. *Honey from the Rock: An Introduction to Jewish Mysticism*. Woodstock, Vt.: Jewish Lights Publishing, 1999.

———. *The Way Into Jewish Mystical Tradition*. Woodstock, Vt.: Jewish Lights Publishing, 2004.

Laitman, Michael. *Awakening to Kabbalah: The Guiding Light of Spiritual Fulfillment*. Woodstock, Vt.: Jewish Lights Publishing, 2006.

Matt, Daniel. *The Essential Kabbalah*. San Francisco: HarperSanFrancisco, 1996.

———. *Zohar: Annotated and Explained*. Woodstock, Vt.: SkyLight Paths Publishing, 2002.

Scholem, Gershom. *Kabbalah*. New York: Times Books, 1987.

———. *Major Trends in Jewish Mysticism*. New York: Schocken, 1995.

Meditation

The Handbook of Jewish Meditation Practices
A Guide for Enriching the Sabbath and Other Days of Your Life
By Rabbi David A. Cooper
Easy-to-learn meditation techniques. 6 x 9, 208 pp, Quality PB, ISBN 1-58023-102-0 **$16.95**

Discovering Jewish Meditation: Instruction & Guidance for Learning an Ancient
Spiritual Practice *By Nan Fink Gefen, Ph.D.* 6 x 9, 208 pp, Quality PB, ISBN 1-58023-067-9 **$16.95**

A Heart of Stillness: A Complete Guide to Learning the Art of Meditation
By Rabbi David A. Cooper 5½ x 8½, 272 pp, Quality PB, ISBN 1-893361-03-9 **$16.95**
(A SkyLight Paths book)

Meditation from the Heart of Judaism: Today's Teachers Share Their
Practices, Techniques, and Faith *Edited by Avram Davis*
6 x 9, 256 pp, Quality PB, ISBN 1-58023-049-0 **$16.95**

Silence, Simplicity & Solitude: A Complete Guide to Spiritual Retreat at Home
By Rabbi David A. Cooper 5½ x 8½, 336 pp, Quality PB, ISBN 1-893361-04-7 **$16.95**
(A SkyLight Paths book)

The Way of Flame: A Guide to the Forgotten Mystical Tradition of Jewish
Meditation *By Avram Davis* 4½ x 8, 176 pp, Quality PB, ISBN 1-58023-060-1 **$15.95**

Ritual/Sacred Practice/Journaling

The Jewish Dream Book: The Key to Opening the Inner Meaning of
Your Dreams *By Vanessa L. Ochs with Elizabeth Ochs; Full-color illus. by Kristina Swarner*
Instructions for how modern people can perform ancient Jewish dream practices and dream interpretations drawn from the Jewish wisdom tradition. For anyone who wants to understand their dreams—and themselves.
8 x 8, 120 pp, Full-color illus., Deluxe PB w/flaps, ISBN 1-58023-132-2 **$16.95**

The Jewish Journaling Book: How to Use Jewish Tradition to Write
Your Life & Explore Your Soul *By Janet Ruth Falon*
Details the history of Jewish journaling throughout biblical and modern times, and teaches specific journaling techniques to help you create and maintain a vital journal, from a Jewish perspective. 8 x 8, 304 pp, Deluxe PB w/flaps, ISBN 1-58023-203-5 **$18.99**

The Book of Jewish Sacred Practices: CLAL's Guide to Everyday & Holiday
Rituals & Blessings *Edited by Rabbi Irwin Kula and Vanessa L. Ochs, Ph.D.*
6 x 9, 368 pp, Quality PB, ISBN 1-58023-152-7 **$18.95**

Jewish Ritual: A Brief Introduction for Christians
By Rabbi Kerry M. Olitzky and Rabbi Daniel Judson
5½ x 8½, 144 pp, Quality PB, ISBN 1-58023-210-8 **$14.99**

The Rituals & Practices of a Jewish Life: A Handbook for Personal
Spiritual Renewal *Edited by Rabbi Kerry M. Olitzky and Rabbi Daniel Judson*
6 x 9, 272 pp, illus., Quality PB, ISBN 1-58023-169-1 **$18.95**

Children's Books

What You Will See Inside a Synagogue
By Rabbi Lawrence A. Hoffman and Dr. Ron Wolfson; Full-color photos by Bill Aron
A colorful, fun-to-read introduction that explains the ways and whys of Jewish worship and religious life. Full-page photos; concise but informative descriptions of the objects used, the clergy and laypeople who have specific roles, and much more. For ages 6 & up.
8½ x 10½, 32 pp, Full-color photos, Hardcover, ISBN 1-59473-012-1 **$17.99** (A SkyLight Paths book)

Because Nothing Looks Like God
By Lawrence and Karen Kushner
What is God like? Introduces children to the possibilities of spiritual life. Real-life examples of happiness and sadness invite us to explore, together with our children, the questions we all have about God.
11 x 8½, 32 pp, Full-color illus., Hardcover, ISBN 1-58023-092-X **$16.95** For ages 4 & up

Also Available: **Because Nothing Looks Like God Teacher's Guide**
8½ x 11, 22 pp, PB, ISBN 1-58023-140-3 **$6.95** For ages 5–8

Board Book Companions to Because Nothing Looks Like God
5 x 5, 24 pp, Full-color illus., SkyLight Paths Board Books For ages 0–4

What Does God Look Like? ISBN 1-893361-23-3 **$7.95**
How Does God Make Things Happen? ISBN 1-893361-24-1 **$7.95**
Where Is God? ISBN 1-893361-17-9 **$7.99**

The 11th Commandment: Wisdom from Our Children
By The Children of America
"If there were an Eleventh Commandment, what would it be?" Children of many religious denominations across America answer in their own drawings and words.
8 x 10, 48 pp, Full-color illus., Hardcover, ISBN 1-879045-46-X **$16.95** For all ages

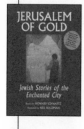

Jerusalem of Gold: Jewish Stories of the Enchanted City
Retold by Howard Schwartz. Full-color illus. by Neil Waldman.
A beautiful and engaging collection of historical and legendary stories for children. Based on Talmud, midrash, Jewish folklore, and mystical and Hasidic sources.
8 x 10, 64 pp, Full-color illus., Hardcover, ISBN 1-58023-149-7 **$18.95** For ages 7 & up

The Book of Miracles: A Young Person's Guide to Jewish Spiritual Awareness
By Lawrence Kushner. All-new illustrations by the author.
6 x 9, 96 pp, 2-color illus., Hardcover, ISBN 1-879045-78-8 **$16.95** For ages 9–13

In Our Image: God's First Creatures
By Nancy Sohn Swartz
9 x 12, 32 pp, Full-color illus., Hardcover, ISBN 1-879045-99-0 **$16.95** For ages 4 & up

Also Available as a Board Book: **How Did the Animals Help God?**
5 x 5, 24 pp, Board, Full-color illus., ISBN 1-59473-044-X **$7.99** For ages 0–4 (A SkyLight Paths book)

From SKYLIGHT PATHS PUBLISHING

Becoming Me: A Story of Creation
By Martin Boroson. Full-color illus. by Christopher Gilvan-Cartwright.
Told in the personal "voice" of the Creator, a story about creation and relationship that is about each one of us.
8 x 10, 32 pp, Full-color illus., Hardcover, ISBN 1-893361-11-X **$16.95** For ages 4 & up

Ten Amazing People: And How They Changed the World
By Maura D. Shaw. Foreword by Dr. Robert Coles. Full-color illus. by Stephen Marchesi.
Black Elk • Dorothy Day • Malcolm X • Mahatma Gandhi • Martin Luther King, Jr. • Mother Teresa • Janusz Korczak • Desmond Tutu • Thich Nhat Hanh • Albert Schweitzer.
8½ x 11, 48 pp, Full-color illus., Hardcover, ISBN 1-893361-47-0 **$17.95** For ages 7 & up

Where Does God Live? By August Gold and Matthew J. Perlman
Helps young readers develop a personal understanding of God.
10 x 8½, 32 pp, Full-color photo illus., Quality PB, ISBN 1-893361-39-X **$8.99** For ages 3–6

Current Events/History

The Story of the Jews: A 4,000-Year Adventure—A Graphic History Book
Written & illustrated by Stan Mack
Witty, illustrated narrative of all the major happenings from biblical times to the
twenty-first century.   6 x 9, 288 pp, illus., Quality PB, ISBN 1-58023-155-1 **$16.95**

Hannah Senesh: Her Life and Diary, the First Complete Edition
By Hannah Senesh; Foreword by Marge Piercy; Preface by Eitan Senesh
6 x 9, 352 pp, Hardcover, ISBN 1-58023-212-4 **$24.99**

The Jewish Prophet: Visionary Words from Moses and Miriam to Henrietta Szold
and A. J. Heschel   By Rabbi Michael J. Shire
6½ x 8½, 128 pp, 123 full-color illus., Hardcover, ISBN 1-58023-168-3 **Special gift price $14.95**

Shared Dreams: Martin Luther King, Jr. & the Jewish Community
By Rabbi Marc Schneier. Preface by Martin Luther King III.
6 x 9, 240 pp, Hardcover, ISBN 1-58023-062-8 **$24.95**

"Who Is a Jew?": Conversations, Not Conclusions   By Meryl Hyman
6 x 9, 272 pp, Quality PB, ISBN 1-58023-052-0 **$16.95**

Ecology

Ecology & the Jewish Spirit: Where Nature & the Sacred Meet
Edited by Ellen Bernstein   6 x 9, 288 pp, Quality PB, ISBN 1-58023-082-2 **$16.95**

Torah of the Earth: Exploring 4,000 Years of Ecology in Jewish Thought
Vol. 1: Biblical Israel: One Land, One People; Rabbinic Judaism: One People, Many Lands
Vol. 2: Zionism: One Land, Two Peoples; Eco-Judaism: One Earth, Many Peoples
Edited by Rabbi Arthur Waskow
Vol. 1: 6 x 9, 272 pp, Quality PB, ISBN 1-58023-086-5 **$19.95**
Vol. 2: 6 x 9, 336 pp, Quality PB, ISBN 1-58023-087-3 **$19.95**

The Way Into Judaism and the Environment
By Jeremy Benstein, PhD
6 x 9, 225 pp (est.), Hardcover, ISBN 1-58023-268-X **$24.99**

Grief/Healing

Against the Dying of the Light: A Parent's Story of Love, Loss and Hope
By Leonard Fein
5½ x 8½, 176 pp, Quality PB, ISBN 1-58023-197-7 **$15.99;** Hardcover, ISBN 1-58023-110-1 **$19.95**

Grief in Our Seasons: A Mourner's Kaddish Companion   By Rabbi Kerry M. Olitzky
4½ x 6½, 448 pp, Quality PB, ISBN 1-879045-55-9 **$15.95**

Healing of Soul, Healing of Body: Spiritual Leaders Unfold the Strength & Solace
in Psalms   Edited by Rabbi Simkha Y. Weintraub, C.S.W.
6 x 9, 128 pp, 2-color illus. text, Quality PB, ISBN 1-879045-31-1 **$14.99**

Jewish Paths toward Healing and Wholeness: A Personal Guide to Dealing with
Suffering   By Rabbi Kerry M. Olitzky. Foreword by Debbie Friedman.
6 x 9, 192 pp, Quality PB, ISBN 1-58023-068-7 **$15.95**

Mourning & Mitzvah, 2nd Edition: A Guided Journal for Walking the Mourner's
Path through Grief to Healing   By Anne Brener, L.C.S.W.
7½ x 9, 304 pp, Quality PB, ISBN 1-58023-113-6 **$19.95**

The Perfect Stranger's Guide to Funerals and Grieving Practices
A Guide to Etiquette in Other People's Religious Ceremonies   Edited by Stuart M. Matlins
6 x 9, 240 pp, Quality PB, ISBN 1-893361-20-9 **$16.95**   (A SkyLight Paths book)

Tears of Sorrow, Seeds of Hope: A Jewish Spiritual Companion for Infertility and
Pregnancy Loss   By Rabbi Nina Beth Cardin
6 x 9, 192 pp, Hardcover, ISBN 1-58023-017-2 **$19.95**

A Time to Mourn, A Time to Comfort, 2nd Edition: A Guide to Jewish
Bereavement and Comfort   By Dr. Ron Wolfson
7 x 9, 336 pp, Quality PB, ISBN 1-58023-253-1 **$19.99**

When a Grandparent Dies: A Kid's Own Remembering Workbook for Dealing
with Shiva and the Year Beyond   By Nechama Liss-Levinson, Ph.D.
8 x 10, 48 pp, 2-color text, Hardcover, ISBN 1-879045-44-3 **$15.95** For ages 7–13

Theology/Philosophy

Aspects of Rabbinic Theology
By Solomon Schechter. New Introduction by Dr. Neil Gillman.
6 x 9, 448 pp, Quality PB, ISBN 1-879045-24-9 **$19.95**

Broken Tablets: Restoring the Ten Commandments and Ourselves
Edited by Rachel S. Mikva. Introduction by Lawrence Kushner. Afterword by Arnold Jacob Wolf.
6 x 9, 192 pp, Quality PB, ISBN 1-58023-158-6 **$16.95**; Hardcover, ISBN 1-58023-066-0 **$21.95**

Creating an Ethical Jewish Life
A Practical Introduction to Classic Teachings on How to Be a Jew
By Dr. Byron L. Sherwin and Seymour J. Cohen
6 x 9, 336 pp, Quality PB, ISBN 1-58023-114-4 **$19.95**

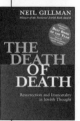

The Death of Death: Resurrection and Immortality in Jewish Thought
By Dr. Neil Gillman 6 x 9, 336 pp, Quality PB, ISBN 1-58023-081-4 **$18.95**

Evolving Halakhah: A Progressive Approach to Traditional Jewish Law
By Rabbi Dr. Moshe Zemer
6 x 9, 480 pp, Quality PB, ISBN 1-58023-127-6 **$29.95**; Hardcover, ISBN 1-58023-002-4 **$40.00**

Hasidic Tales: Annotated & Explained
By Rabbi Rami Shapiro. Foreword by Andrew Harvey, SkyLight Illuminations series editor.
5½ x 8½, 240 pp, Quality PB, ISBN 1-893361-86-1 **$16.95** (A SkyLight Paths Book)

A Heart of Many Rooms: Celebrating the Many Voices within Judaism
By Dr. David Hartman 6 x 9, 352 pp, Quality PB, ISBN 1-58023-156-X **$19.95**

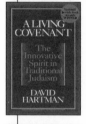

The Hebrew Prophets: Selections Annotated & Explained
Translation & Annotation by Rabbi Rami Shapiro. Foreword by Zalman M. Schachter-Shalomi
5½ x 8½, 224 pp, Quality PB, ISBN 1-59473-037-7 **$16.99** (A SkyLight Paths book)

Keeping Faith with the Psalms: Deepen Your Relationship with God Using the
Book of Psalms By Daniel F. Polish 6 x 9, 320 pp, Quality PB, ISBN 1-58023-300-7 **$18.99**;
Hardcover, ISBN 1-58023-179-9 **$24.95**

The Last Trial
On the Legends and Lore of the Command to Abraham to Offer Isaac as a Sacrifice
By Shalom Spiegel. New Introduction by Judah Goldin.
6 x 9, 208 pp, Quality PB, ISBN 1-879045-29-X **$18.95**

A Living Covenant: The Innovative Spirit in Traditional Judaism
By Dr. David Hartman 6 x 9, 368 pp, Quality PB, ISBN 1-58023-011-3 **$18.95**

Love and Terror in the God Encounter
The Theological Legacy of Rabbi Joseph B. Soloveitchik
By Dr. David Hartman
6 x 9, 240 pp, Quality PB, ISBN 1-58023-176-4 **$19.95**; Hardcover, ISBN 1-58023-112-8 **$25.00**

The Personhood of God: Biblical Theology, Human Faith and the Divine Image
By Dr. Yochanan Muffs; Foreword by Dr. David Hartman
6 x 9, 240 pp, Hardcover, ISBN 1-58023-265-5 **$24.99**

The Spirit of Renewal: Finding Faith after the Holocaust
By Rabbi Edward Feld 6 x 9, 224 pp, Quality PB, ISBN 1-879045-40-0 **$16.95**

Tormented Master: The Life and Spiritual Quest of Rabbi Nahman of Bratslav
By Dr. Arthur Green 6 x 9, 416 pp, Quality PB, ISBN 1-879045-11-7 **$19.99**

Your Word Is Fire: The Hasidic Masters on Contemplative Prayer
Edited and translated by Dr. Arthur Green and Barry W. Holtz
6 x 9, 160 pp, Quality PB, ISBN 1-879045-25-7 **$15.95**

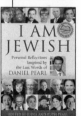

I Am Jewish
Personal Reflections Inspired by the Last Words of Daniel Pearl
Almost 150 Jews—both famous and not—from all walks of life, from all around
the world, write about Identity, Heritage, Covenant / Chosenness and Faith,
Humanity and Ethnicity, and *Tikkun Olam* and Justice.
Edited by Judea and Ruth Pearl
6 x 9, 304 pp, Deluxe PB w/flaps, ISBN 1-58023-259-0 **$18.99**; Hardcover, ISBN 1-58023-183-7 **$24.99**
Download a free copy of the *I Am Jewish Teacher's Guide* at our website:
www.jewishlights.com

Spirituality/The Way Into... Series

The Way Into... Series offers an accessible and highly usable "guided tour" of the Jewish faith, people, history and beliefs—in total, an introduction to Judaism that will enable you to understand and interact with the sacred texts of the Jewish tradition. Each volume is written by a leading contemporary scholar and teacher, and explores one key aspect of Judaism. *The Way Into...* enables all readers to achieve a real sense of Jewish cultural literacy through guided study.

The Way Into Encountering God in Judaism   *By Neil Gillman*
6 x 9, 240 pp, Quality PB, ISBN 1-58023-199-3 **$18.99**; Hardcover, ISBN 1-58023-025-3 **$21.95**

Also Available: **The Jewish Approach to God: A Brief Introduction for Christians**
By Neil Gillman 5½ x 8½, 192 pp, Quality PB, ISBN 1-58023-190-X **$16.95**

The Way Into Jewish Mystical Tradition   *By Lawrence Kushner*
6 x 9, 224 pp, Quality PB, ISBN 1-58023-200-0 **$18.99**; Hardcover, ISBN 1-58023-029-6 **$21.95**

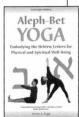

The Way Into Jewish Prayer   *By Lawrence A. Hoffman*
6 x 9, 224 pp, Quality PB, ISBN 1-58023-201-9 **$18.99**; Hardcover, ISBN 1-58023-027-X **$21.95**

The Way Into the Relationship between Jews and Non-Jews: Searching for Boundaries and Bridges   *By Michael A. Signer, PhD*
6 x 9, 225 pp (est.), Hardcover, ISBN 1-58023-267-1 **$24.99**

The Way Into Judaism and the Environment   *By Jeremy Benstein, PhD*
6 x 9, 225 pp (est.), Hardcover, ISBN 1-58023-268-X **$24.99**

The Way Into *Tikkun Olam* (Repairing the World)   *By Elliot N. Dorff*
6 x 9, 320 pp, Hardcover, ISBN 1-58023-269-8 **$24.99**

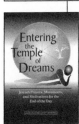

The Way Into Torah   *By Norman J. Cohen*
6 x 9, 176 pp, Quality PB, ISBN 1-58023-198-5 **$16.99**; Hardcover, ISBN 1-58023-028-8 **$21.95**

 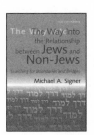  

Spirituality and Wellness

Aleph-Bet Yoga
Embodying the Hebrew Letters for Physical and Spiritual Well-Being
By Steven A. Rapp. Foreword by Tamar Frankiel, Ph.D., and Judy Greenfeld. Preface by Hart Lazer
7 x 10, 128 pp, b/w photos, Quality PB, Layflat binding, ISBN 1-58023-162-4 **$16.95**

Entering the Temple of Dreams
Jewish Prayers, Movements, and Meditations for the End of the Day
By Tamar Frankiel, Ph.D., and Judy Greenfeld
7 x 10, 192 pp, illus., Quality PB, ISBN 1-58023-079-2 **$16.95**

Jewish Paths toward Healing and Wholeness: A Personal Guide to Dealing with Suffering   *By Rabbi Kerry M. Olitzky. Foreword by Debbie Friedman.*
6 x 9, 192 pp, Quality PB, ISBN 1-58023-068-7 **$15.95**

Minding the Temple of the Soul
Balancing Body, Mind, and Spirit through Traditional Jewish Prayer, Movement, and Meditation   *By Tamar Frankiel, Ph.D., and Judy Greenfeld*
7 x 10, 184 pp, illus., Quality PB, ISBN 1-879045-64-8 **$16.95**
Audiotape of the Blessings and Meditations: 60 min. **$9.95**
Videotape of the Movements and Meditations: 46 min. **$20.00**

Spirituality/Lawrence Kushner

Filling Words with Light: Hasidic and Mystical Reflections on Jewish Prayer
By Lawrence Kushner and Nehemia Polen
Reflects on the joy, gratitude, mystery and awe embedded in traditional prayers and blessings, and shows how you can imbue these familiar sacred words with your own sense of holiness. 5½ x 8½, 176 pp, Hardcover, ISBN 1-58023-216-7 **$21.99**

The Book of Letters: A Mystical Hebrew Alphabet
Popular Hardcover Edition, 6 x 9, 80 pp, 2-color text, ISBN 1-879045-00-1 **$24.95**
Collector's Limited Edition, 9 x 12, 80 pp, gold foil embossed pages, w/limited edition silkscreened print, ISBN 1-879045-04-4 **$349.00**

The Book of Miracles: A Young Person's Guide to Jewish Spiritual Awareness
6 x 9, 96 pp, 2-color illus., Hardcover, ISBN 1-879045-78-8 **$16.95** *For ages 9–13*

The Book of Words: Talking Spiritual Life, Living Spiritual Talk
6 x 9, 160 pp, Quality PB, ISBN 1-58023-020-2 **$16.95**

Eyes Remade for Wonder: A Lawrence Kushner Reader   *Introduction by Thomas Moore*
6 x 9, 240 pp, Quality PB, ISBN 1-58023-042-3 **$18.95;** Hardcover, ISBN 1-58023-014-8 **$23.95**

God Was in This Place & I, i Did Not Know
Finding Self, Spirituality and Ultimate Meaning   6 x 9, 192 pp, Quality PB, ISBN 1-879045-33-8 **$16.95**

Honey from the Rock: An Introduction to Jewish Mysticism
6 x 9, 176 pp, Quality PB, ISBN 1-58023-073-3 **$16.95**

Invisible Lines of Connection: Sacred Stories of the Ordinary
5½ x 8½, 160 pp, Quality PB, ISBN 1-879045-98-2 **$15.95**

Jewish Spirituality—A Brief Introduction for Christians
5¼ x 8½, 112 pp, Quality PB Original, ISBN 1-58023-150-0 **$12.95**

The River of Light: Jewish Mystical Awareness 6 x 9, 192 pp, Quality PB, ISBN 1-58023-096-2 **$16.95**

The Way Into Jewish Mystical Tradition
6 x 9, 224 pp, Quality PB, ISBN 1-58023-200-0 **$18.99;** Hardcover, ISBN 1-58023-029-6 **$21.95**

Spirituality/Prayer

Pray Tell: A Hadassah Guide to Jewish Prayer
By Rabbi Jules Harlow, with contributions from Tamara Cohen, Rochelle Furstenberg, Rabbi Daniel Gordis, Leora Tanenbaum, and many others
Enriched with insight and wisdom from a broad variety of viewpoints.
8½ x 11, 400 pp, Quality PB, ISBN 1-58023-163-2 **$29.95**

My People's Prayer Book Series

Traditional Prayers, Modern Commentaries   *Edited by Rabbi Lawrence A. Hoffman*
Provides diverse and exciting commentary to the traditional liturgy, helping modern men and women find new wisdom in Jewish prayer, and bring liturgy into their lives. Each book includes Hebrew text, modern translation, and commentaries from all perspectives of the Jewish world.

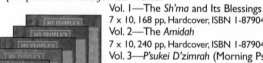

Vol. 1—The *Sh'ma* and Its Blessings
7 x 10, 168 pp, Hardcover, ISBN 1-879045-79-6 **$24.99**
Vol. 2—The *Amidah*
7 x 10, 240 pp, Hardcover, ISBN 1-879045-80-X **$24.95**
Vol. 3—*P'sukei D'zimrah* (Morning Psalms)
7 x 10, 240 pp, Hardcover, ISBN 1-879045-81-8 **$24.95**
Vol. 4—*Seder K'riat Hatorah* (The Torah Service)
7 x 10, 264 pp, Hardcover, ISBN 1-879045-82-6 **$23.95**
Vol. 5—*Birkhot Hashachar* (Morning Blessings)
7 x 10, 240 pp, Hardcover, ISBN 1-879045-83-4 **$24.95**
Vol. 6—*Tachanun* and Concluding Prayers
7 x 10, 240 pp, Hardcover, ISBN 1-879045-84-2 **$24.95**
Vol. 7—Shabbat at Home
7 x 10, 240 pp, Hardcover, ISBN 1-879045-85-0 **$24.95**
Vol. 8—*Kabbalat Shabbat* (Welcoming Shabbat in the Synagogue)
7 x 10, 240 pp, Hardcover, ISBN 1-58023-121-7 **$24.99**
Vol. 9—Welcoming the Night: *Minchah* and *Ma'ariv* (Afternoon and Evening Prayer) 7 x 10, 272 pp, Hardcover, ISBN 1-58023-262-0 **$24.99**

Spirituality/Women's Interest

The Quotable Jewish Woman: Wisdom, Inspiration & Humor from the Mind & Heart *Edited and compiled by Elaine Bernstein Partnow*
The definitive collection of ideas, reflections, humor, and wit of over 300 Jewish women.
6 x 9, 496 pp, Hardcover, ISBN 1-58023-193-4 **$29.99**

Lifecycles, Vol. 1: Jewish Women on Life Passages & Personal Milestones
Edited and with introductions by Rabbi Debra Orenstein 6 x 9, 480 pp, Quality PB, ISBN 1-58023-018-0 **$19.95**
Lifecycles, Vol. 2: Jewish Women on Biblical Themes in Contemporary Life
Edited and with introductions by Rabbi Debra Orenstein and Rabbi Jane Rachel Litman
6 x 9, 464 pp, Quality PB, ISBN 1-58023-019-9 **$19.95**

Moonbeams: A Hadassah Rosh Hodesh Guide *Edited by Carol Diament, Ph.D.*
8½ x 11, 240 pp, Quality PB, ISBN 1-58023-099-7 **$20.00**

ReVisions: Seeing Torah through a Feminist Lens *By Rabbi Elyse Goldstein*
5½ x 8½, 224 pp, Quality PB, ISBN 1-58023-117-9 **$16.95**

White Fire: A Portrait of Women Spiritual Leaders in America
By Rabbi Malka Drucker. Photographs by Gay Block.
7 x 10, 320 pp, 30+ b/w photos, Hardcover, ISBN 1-893361-64-0 **$24.95** *(A SkyLight Paths book)*

Women of the Wall: Claiming Sacred Ground at Judaism's Holy Site
Edited by Phyllis Chesler and Rivka Haut 6 x 9, 496 pp, b/w photos, Hardcover, ISBN 1-58023-161-6 **$34.95**

The Women's Haftarah Commentary: New Insights from Women Rabbis on the 54 Weekly Haftarah Portions, the 5 Megillot & Special Shabbatot
Edited by Rabbi Elyse Goldstein 6 x 9, 560 pp, Hardcover, ISBN 1-58023-133-0 **$39.99**

The Women's Torah Commentary: New Insights from Women Rabbis on the 54 Weekly Torah Portions *Edited by Rabbi Elyse Goldstein*
6 x 9, 496 pp, Hardcover, ISBN 1-58023-076-8 **$34.95**

The Year Mom Got Religion: One Woman's Midlife Journey into Judaism
By Lee Meyerhoff Hendler 6 x 9, 208 pp, Quality PB, ISBN 1-58023-070-9 **$15.95**

See Holidays for *The Women's Passover Companion: Women's Reflections on the Festival of Freedom* and *The Women's Seder Sourcebook: Rituals & Readings for Use at the Passover Seder.* Also see Bar/Bat Mitzvah for *The JGirl's Guide: The Young Jewish Woman's Handbook for Coming of Age.*

Travel

Israel—A Spiritual Travel Guide, 2nd Edition
A Companion for the Modern Jewish Pilgrim
By Rabbi Lawrence A. Hoffman 4¾ x 10, 256 pp, Quality PB, illus., ISBN 1-58023-261-2 **$18.99**
Also Available: **The Israel Mission Leader's Guide** ISBN 1-58023-085-7 **$4.95**

12 Steps

100 Blessings Every Day Daily Twelve Step Recovery Affirmations, Exercises for Personal Growth & Renewal Reflecting Seasons of the Jewish Year
By Rabbi Kerry M. Olitzky. Foreword by Rabbi Neil Gillman.
One-day-at-a-time monthly format. Reflects on the rhythm of the Jewish calendar to bring insight to recovery from addictions.
4½ x 6¼, 432 pp, Quality PB, ISBN 1-879045-30-3 **$15.99**

Recovery from Codependence: A Jewish Twelve Steps Guide to Healing Your Soul
By Rabbi Kerry M. Olitzky 6 x 9, 160 pp, Quality PB, ISBN 1-879045-32-X **$13.95**

Renewed Each Day: Daily Twelve Step Recovery Meditations Based on the Bible
By Rabbi Kerry M. Olitzky and Aaron Z.
Vol. 1—Genesis & Exodus: 6 x 9, 224 pp, Quality PB, ISBN 1-879045-12-5 **$14.95**
Vol. 2—Leviticus, Numbers & Deuteronomy: 6 x 9, 280 pp, Quality PB, ISBN 1-879045-13-3 **$18.99**

Twelve Jewish Steps to Recovery: A Personal Guide to Turning from Alcoholism & Other Addictions—Drugs, Food, Gambling, Sex...
By Rabbi Kerry M. Olitzky and Stuart A. Copans, M.D. Preface by Abraham J. Twerski, M.D.
6 x 9, 144 pp, Quality PB, ISBN 1-879045-09-5 **$14.95**

Spirituality

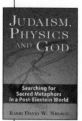

Does the Soul Survive? A Jewish Journey to Belief in Afterlife, Past Lives & Living with Purpose *By Rabbi Elie Kaplan Spitz. Foreword by Brian L Weiss, M.D.*
Spitz relates his own experiences and those shared with him by people he has worked with as a rabbi, and shows us that belief in afterlife and past lives, so often approached with reluctance, is in fact true to Jewish tradition.
6 x 9, 288 pp, Quality PB, ISBN 1-58023-165-9 **$16.95**; Hardcover, ISBN 1-58023-094-6 **$21.95**

First Steps to a New Jewish Spirit: Reb Zalman's Guide to Recapturing the Intimacy & Ecstasy in Your Relationship with God
By Rabbi Zalman M. Schachter-Shalomi with Donald Gropman
An extraordinary spiritual handbook that restores psychic and physical vigor by introducing us to new models and alternative ways of practicing Judaism. Offers meditation and contemplation exercises for enriching the most important aspects of everyday life. 6 x 9, 144 pp, Quality PB, ISBN 1-58023-182-9 **$16.95**

God in Our Relationships: Spirituality between People from the Teachings of Martin Buber *By Rabbi Dennis S. Ross*
On the eightieth anniversary of Buber's classic work, we can discover new answers to critical issues in our lives. Inspiring examples from Ross's own life—as congregational rabbi, father, hospital chaplain, social worker, and husband—illustrate Buber's difficult-to-understand ideas about how we encounter God and each other. 5½ x 8¼, 160 pp, Quality PB, ISBN 1-58023-147-0 **$16.95**

Judaism, Physics and God: Searching for Sacred Metaphors in a Post-Einstein World *By Rabbi David W. Nelson*
In clear, non-technical terms, this provocative fusion of religion and science examines the great theories of modern physics to find new ways for contemporary people to express their spiritual beliefs and thoughts.
6 x 9, 352 pp, Hardcover, ISBN 1-58023-252-3 **$24.99**

The Jewish Lights Spirituality Handbook: A Guide to Understanding, Exploring & Living a Spiritual Life *Edited by Stuart M. Matlins*
What exactly is "Jewish" about spirituality? How do I make it a part of my life? Fifty of today's foremost spiritual leaders share their ideas and experience with us.
6 x 9, 456 pp, Quality PB, ISBN 1-58023-093-8 **$19.95**; Hardcover, ISBN 1-58023-100-4 **$24.95**

Bringing the Psalms to Life: How to Understand and Use the Book of Psalms
By Dr. Daniel F. Polish
6 x 9, 208 pp, Quality PB, ISBN 1-58023-157-8 **$16.95**; Hardcover, ISBN 1-58023-077-6 **$21.95**

God & the Big Bang: Discovering Harmony between Science & Spirituality
By Dr. Daniel C. Matt 6 x 9, 216 pp, Quality PB, ISBN 1-879045-89-3 **$16.95**

Godwrestling—Round 2: Ancient Wisdom, Future Paths
By Rabbi Arthur Waskow 6 x 9, 352 pp, Quality PB, ISBN 1-879045-72-9 **$18.95**

One God Clapping: The Spiritual Path of a Zen Rabbi *By Rabbi Alan Lew with Sherril Jaffe*
5½ x 8¼, 336 pp, Quality PB, ISBN 1-58023-115-2 **$16.95**

The Path of Blessing: Experiencing the Energy and Abundance of the Divine
By Rabbi Marcia Prager 5½ x 8¼, 240 pp., Quality PB, ISBN 1-58023-148-9 **$16.95**

Six Jewish Spiritual Paths: A Rationalist Looks at Spirituality *By Rabbi Rifat Sonsino*
6 x 9, 208 pp, Quality PB, ISBN 1-58023-167-5 **$16.95**; Hardcover, ISBN 1-58023-095-4 **$21.95**

Soul Judaism: Dancing with God into a New Era
By Rabbi Wayne Dosick 5½ x 8¼, 304 pp, Quality PB, ISBN 1-58023-053-9 **$16.95**

Stepping Stones to Jewish Spiritual Living: Walking the Path Morning, Noon, and Night *By Rabbi James L Mirel and Karen Bonnell Werth*
6 x 9, 240 pp, Quality PB, ISBN 1-58023-074-1 **$16.95**; Hardcover, ISBN 1-58023-003-2 **$21.95**

There Is No Messiah ... and You're It: The Stunning Transformation of Judaism's Most Provocative Idea *By Rabbi Robert N. Levine, D.D.*
6 x 9, 192 pp, Quality PB, ISBN 1-58023-255-8 **$16.99**; Hardcover, ISBN 1-58023-173-X **$21.95**

These Are the Words: A Vocabulary of Jewish Spiritual Life *By Dr. Arthur Green*
6 x 9, 304 pp, Quality PB, ISBN 1-58023-107-1 **$18.95**

Inspiration

God in All Moments
Mystical & Practical Spiritual Wisdom from Hasidic Masters
Edited and translated by Or N. Rose with Ebn D. Leader
Hasidic teachings on how to be mindful in religious practice and cultivating every-day ethical behavior—*hanhagot*. 5½ x 8½, 192 pp, Quality PB, ISBN 1-58023-186-1 **$16.95**

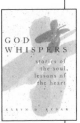

Our Dance with God: Finding Prayer, Perspective and Meaning in the Stories of Our Lives *By Karyn D. Kedar*
Inspiring spiritual insight to guide you on your life journeys and teach you to live and thrive in two conflicting worlds: the rational/material and the spiritual.
6 x 9, 176 pp, Quality PB, ISBN 1-58023-202-7 **$16.99**

Also Available: **The Dance of the Dolphin** (Hardcover edition of *Our Dance with God*)
6 x 9, 176 pp, Hardcover, ISBN 1-58023-154-3 **$19.95**

The Empty Chair: Finding Hope and Joy—Timeless Wisdom from a Hasidic Master, Rebbe Nachman of Breslov *Adapted by Moshe Mykoff and the Breslov Research Institute*
4 x 6, 128 pp, 2-color text, Deluxe PB w/flaps, ISBN 1-879045-67-2 **$9.95**

The Gentle Weapon: Prayers for Everyday and Not-So-Everyday Moments—Timeless Wisdom from the Teachings of the Hasidic Master, Rebbe Nachman of Breslov
Adapted by Moshe Mykoff and S. C. Mizrahi, together with the Breslov Research Institute
4 x 6, 144 pp, 2-color text, Deluxe PB w/flaps, ISBN 1-58023-022-9 **$9.95**

God Whispers: Stories of the Soul, Lessons of the Heart *By Karyn D. Kedar*
6 x 9, 176 pp, Quality PB, ISBN 1-58023-088-1 **$15.95**

An Orphan in History: One Man's Triumphant Search for His Jewish Roots
By Paul Cowan. Afterword by Rachel Cowan. 6 x 9, 288 pp, Quality PB, ISBN 1-58023-135-7 **$16.95**

Restful Reflections: Nighttime Inspiration to Calm the Soul, Based on Jewish Wisdom
By Rabbi Kerry M. Olitzky & Rabbi Lori Forman 4½ x 6½, 448 pp, Quality PB, ISBN 1-58023-091-1 **$15.95**

Sacred Intentions: Daily Inspiration to Strengthen the Spirit, Based on Jewish Wisdom
By Rabbi Kerry M. Olitzky and Rabbi Lori Forman 4½ x 6½, 448 pp, Quality PB, ISBN 1-58023-061-X **$15.95**

Kabbalah/Mysticism/Enneagram

Awakening to Kabbalah: The Guiding Light of Spiritual Fulfillment
By Rav Michael Laitman, PhD
A distinctive, personal and awe-filled introduction to this ancient wisdom tradition.
6 x 9, 192 pp, Hardcover, ISBN 1-58023-264-7 **$21.99**

Seek My Face: A Jewish Mystical Theology
By Dr. Arthur Green
This classic work of contemporary Jewish theology, revised and updated, is a pro-found, deeply personal statement of the lasting truths of Jewish mysticism and the basic faith claims of Judaism. 6 x 9, 304 pp, Quality PB, ISBN 1-58023-130-6 **$19.95**

Zohar: Annotated & Explained
Translation and annotation by Dr. Daniel C. Matt. Foreword by Andrew Harvey
Offers insightful yet unobtrusive commentary to the masterpiece of Jewish mys-ticism. 5½ x 8½, 160 pp, Quality PB, ISBN 1-893361-51-9 **$15.99** *(A SkyLight Paths book)*

Cast in God's Image: Discover Your Personality Type Using the Enneagram and Kabbalah
By Rabbi Howard A. Addison
7 x 9, 176 pp, Quality PB, Layflat binding, 20+ journaling exercises, ISBN 1-58023-124-1 **$16.95**

Ehyeh: A Kabbalah for Tomorrow *By Dr. Arthur Green*
6 x 9, 224 pp, Quality PB, ISBN 1-58023-213-2 **$16.99;** Hardcover, ISBN 1-58023-125-X **$21.95**

The Enneagram and Kabbalah: Reading Your Soul, 2nd Edition
By Rabbi Howard A. Addison 6 x 9, 192 pp, Quality PB, ISBN 1-58023-229-9 **$16.99**

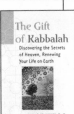

Finding Joy: A Practical Spiritual Guide to Happiness *By Dannel I. Schwartz with Mark Hass*
6 x 9, 192 pp, Quality PB, ISBN 1-58023-009-1 **$14.95**

The Gift of Kabbalah: Discovering the Secrets of Heaven, Renewing Your Life on Earth
By Tamar Frankiel, Ph.D.
6 x 9, 256 pp, Quality PB, ISBN 1-58023-141-1 **$16.95;** Hardcover, ISBN 1-58023-108-X **$21.95**

The Way Into Jewish Mystical Tradition *By Lawrence Kushner*
6 x 9, 224 pp, Quality PB, ISBN 1-58023-200-0 **$18.99;** Hardcover, ISBN 1-58023-029-6 **$21.95**

About Jewish Lights

People of all faiths and backgrounds yearn for books that attract, engage, educate, and spiritually inspire.

Our principal goal is to stimulate thought and help all people learn about who the Jewish People are, where they come from, and what the future can be made to hold. While people of our diverse Jewish heritage are the primary audience, our books speak to people in the Christian world as well and will broaden their understanding of Judaism and the roots of their own faith.

We bring to you authors who are at the forefront of spiritual thought and experience. While each has something different to say, they all say it in a voice that you can hear.

Our books are designed to welcome you and then to engage, stimulate, and inspire. We judge our success not only by whether or not our books are beautiful and commercially successful, but by whether or not they make a difference in your life.

For your information and convenience, at the back of this book we have provided a list of other Jewish Lights books you might find interesting and useful. They cover all the categories of your life:

Bar/Bat Mitzvah	Life Cycle
Bible Study / Midrash	Meditation
Children's Books	Parenting
Congregation Resources	Prayer
Current Events / History	Ritual / Sacred Practice
Ecology	Spirituality
Fiction: Mystery, Science Fiction	Theology / Philosophy
Grief / Healing	Travel
Holidays / Holy Days	Twelve Steps
Inspiration	Women's Interest
Kabbalah / Mysticism / Enneagram	

Stuart M. Matlins, Publisher

Or phone, fax, mail or e-mail to: **JEWISH LIGHTS Publishing**
Sunset Farm Offices, Route 4 • P.O. Box 237 • Woodstock, Vermont 05091
Tel: (802) 457-4000 • Fax: (802) 457-4004 • www.jewishlights.com
Credit card orders: **(800) 962-4544** (8:30AM–5:30PM ET Monday–Friday)
Generous discounts on quantity orders. SATISFACTION GUARANTEED. Prices subject to change.